Life Works and Faith Fits

Life Works and Faith Fits
True Stories for Teens

Lisa-Marie Calderone-Stewart

Saint Mary's Press
Christian Brothers Publications
Winona, Minnesota

Genuine recycled paper with 10% post-consumer waste.
Printed with soy-based ink.

The publishing team included Robert P. Stamschror, development
editor; Laurie A. Berg, copy editor; James H. Gurley, production editor;
Hollace Storkel, typesetter; Rick Korab, cover designer; Maurine R.
Twait, art director; pre-press, printing, and binding by the graphics
division of Saint Mary's Press.

The acknowledgments continue on page 107.

Printed in the United States of America

Printing: 9 8 7 6 5 4 3 2 1

Year: 2007 06 05 04 03 02 01 00 99

ISBN 0-88489-547-5

To Robert T. Massa
1957–1994

We learned so much together:
   the art of the word
   the power of story
   the leverage of analogy
   the humor and humility of self-reflection.
We found God in the simple and the significant.
We kept discovering how life works and how faith fits.
And we celebrated every discovery.

Thank you, Mom (Connie Calderone), for all the joy and fun you bring me! You are so eager to hear about every new story that happens! Your love and laughter and attitude are a model for my life.

Thank you, Dad (Joseph Calderone Sr.), and Τισ ανωεθαι ταυτα γενεστι.

Thank you, Joe, Steve, and David (Calderone), for being marvelous brothers and for creating such wonderful stories for me to write about!

Thank you, Ralph (Stewart), for your love and care, your technical computer assistance, your support, and your perspective. Thank you for sharing life and creating family with me.

Thank you, Ralph (IV) and Michael (Stewart), for growing up so well and for all the love and family richness you bring to Dad and me.

Thank you, Heidi and Marie, Bernadette, Elizabeth, and Barbara (Calderone) for the delight you are! How blessed we are because of you! Thank you, Danny (Croce). You are really the family storyteller!

Thank you, Mike (Dundon) and Fran (Clark).
Thank you, Tim and Mary Beth (Ward).
High school friendships leave an indelible mark.

Thanks also to Nancy and Donna Introcaso, Vince Small, Karen Schulhafer, Ellen Kenny, Sylvia Pramataroff, Eugenia Fernandez, Valerie Pendrick, Jayne Gurrera, Pat Caruso, Jim Hanley, Gerry Appel, Kevin Gudzak, Guy Zanelli, and Rich Fink. All the stories and lessons of life just can't fit into one book!

Thank you, David (Chang). I wish you and I had more stories to tell.

Thank you, Bob (Father Stamschror). You always have faith in me; you always encourage whatever ideas seem to be emerging. You never even think those words, "It can't be done!" You take whatever I give you and make it better.

Thank you, Ken (Bishop Untener). You have had a major influence on my spiritual formation, my ministry, and my life.

Contents

Introduction

I hope you like stories. Because this book is full of them. Some are funny, some are more serious. Some of them are embarrassing (such as the time I asked nine boys to a dance during my sophomore year, and they all said no), but there are some that I am proud of (such as the time I passed my water tests to become a lifeguard and swimming instructor).

Some of the stories involve my friends, some involve my family, and some even involve strangers. Some are stories from my own teen years, some are from my years in college, and some are from when I was a young adult, out of college and on my own. Some stories involve other teenagers I know. But I promise you this: the stories are all true.

Now, I must admit that in some of these stories, I've changed the names of some of the characters (to protect the innocent), and in one or two of them, I've simplified the details—*just a tiny bit*—to make the story less complicated and easier to tell. But very little has been changed—nothing that would really affect the plot or the point. Why am I telling you all this? Because the funny thing is that all my stories seem to be related in some way to the stories of the Bible. Isn't that a strange coincidence? Not really. Believe me, when I was a teenager, I did not study the Bible every day and then ask myself, "Hmm . . . what happened to me today that has scriptural significance?" It was only after I had grown up and had become more active in church ministry that I actually began to take a closer look at the Bible. And as I read the stories and learned about the people in the Bible, I started to say to myself, "This sounds like my life."

Okay, I have never witnessed angels singing and playing harps or offered a burnt animal sacrifice. But even so, the struggles of the people in the Bible are similar to the struggles of people today. We live in a different culture from the days of Abraham and Sarah, and of Joseph and Mary, but we still wonder, "Are things going to turn out okay?" and "What do my friends think about me?" and "Why is this happening to me?" The people in the Bible had the same concerns that we have. Even though the details are different, the basics are similar. In the Bible, teenagers are falling in love, people have fears and worries about the unknown, they have dirty feet, and they have silly arguments. My story is part of the Bible story, and so is yours.

You might be thinking: "Not me. My story isn't in the Bible story. Faith doesn't really fit. Life doesn't really work. Not for me, not like that. I'm not very religious."

Well, you don't have to be "religious" in order to be spiritual. And I'll bet you are more spiritual than you think.

Have you ever looked up at the stars and wondered where they end? That's spiritual, that's meditating on God's magnificent creation.

Have you ever felt trapped in a difficult situation and wondered what you ought to do? That's spiritual, that's moral decision making.

Have you ever become angry watching someone take unfair advantage of another person? That's spiritual, that's developing your sense of Christian justice.

Do you still think that you're not spiritual? Still doubt that life works? Still doubt that faith fits? That's okay. Just read some of the stories in this book—in any order. Just flip through the book and pick a spot.

It's all in the bicycles, the toenails, and the tomato sauce.

Read it. You'll see.

Life works and faith fits.

Look into the Heart

It was the perfect summer day.

For the first time ever, my mom was going to make tomato sauce from fresh tomatoes. And not with just any tomatoes. She was going to use the tomatoes grown from my dad's own garden. We could see it from the kitchen window.

What a perfect project. Our family loves Italian food. We are Italian. I sometimes tell people that we are so Italian that if you prick our skin, it bleeds spaghetti sauce. And now my mom was going to make the perfect sauce.

Well, making tomato sauce from scratch is hard work—a lot of cutting and straining and bubbling and more straining, and making messes and cleaning them up. But my mother was performing a labor of love.

To be honest, I don't recall why I wasn't there by her side, learning the trade of my ancestors. Perhaps I was working that day at my summer-camp job. Perhaps I was having one of my teenage moods, and I didn't want any mother-daughter bonding. Perhaps I wasn't in a tomato frame of mind.

But whatever the reason, when I walked into the house early that evening, I was immediately struck with the results. The smell of tomato sauce reached all the way to the hallway. I could see how much work it had taken, and I felt bad that my mom had done it all by herself. I did want to help out somehow, so I began to wash and dry and put away the dishes and pots that were on the counter, and some glasses and silverware as well.

I don't know how it happened, but one minute I had a glass in my hand, and the next minute I didn't. There was a crash, and glass flew all over the counter, all over the floor, all over the kitchen. I held my breath. I thought my mom was going to become unglued. I thought she was going to yell her head off at me.

But she didn't. She just sighed. And she said, "Well, so much for the tomato sauce." Then she started to pick up pieces of the glass.

At first, I didn't realize what she meant. But when I took a closer look, I saw glass all around the precious tomato sauce, and floating on top of the sauce as well. It was ruined. Even if we tried to take out the pieces we could see, we wouldn't be sure that we had gotten it all. Tiny pieces could be hiding there. I didn't want to ask what it would be like to swallow a sharp piece of hidden glass.

I could tell that my mother was heartbroken. But somehow she wasn't angry with me. What a terrible thing I had done! And yet she still wasn't angry with me. How could that be? I meekly asked her, "Aren't you mad at me?" She quietly replied: "You didn't do it on purpose. You were trying to help. Your heart was in the right place."

It was the only time my mother ever made home-made tomato sauce from garden-fresh tomatoes.

Scripture

Jesus was criticized for not following some of the religious rituals of his day—rituals like washing your arms up to the elbow before eating, sprinkling food from the market with water before eating it, only eating certain types of foods in certain dishes or bowls, and things like that. According to the religious law of the time, violations like these caused a person to be unclean.

Jesus told them, "Don't you see that whatever enters us from outside cannot make us impure? . . . It is what comes out of us that makes us unclean. For it is from within—from our hearts—that evil intentions emerge" (Mark 7:18–21, INT).

Jesus is like my mother. He understands the importance of looking into the heart.

Reflections

Did you ever get in trouble for doing something wrong when your intentions were perfectly innocent, when your heart was in the right place? What was it like?

Did you ever get caught doing something wrong when your intentions were not innocent? Did you then try to talk your way out of it, trying to convince the person in authority that you were perfectly innocent, that your heart was in the right place? What happened? How did you feel afterward?

Did anyone ever do "a terrible thing" to you by mistake? How did you handle it?

Go Back and Make Peace

I was visiting some friends one weekend. My brother David was there, my best friend David from college, and another friend named Ron. One of the days we decided to have dessert at a pastry shop, but it was very crowded, and, as it turned out, we never got to sit down and eat.

As we fought the crowd, my brother noticed this cute figurine on the counter. It was a little baker holding two trays of pastries, one in each hand. In fact, it was a mechanical baker whose head bobbed back and forth and whose arms alternated up and down.

I said, "Oh! Look at the ceramic pastries on his little trays! Aren't they realistic? You could almost eat one!"

My brother corrected me. "Lisa, those are foam. They are like sponges. They aren't ceramic."

"No, I am sure they are ceramic," I insisted.

Well, we took a poll. It was dead even. Two voted for ceramic, and two voted for foam. The problem was that we were too far away to tell. So we pushed through the crowd to get a closer look. We thought that if we could touch them, we would know if they were ceramic or foam.

Now, I don't remember the details of what happened next. I only know that at least one of us got close enough to touch them; at least one of us knocked the whole thing over. And then all of us ran out of that shop in a flash—arguing over who had touched it, who had knocked it over, whose fault it was, and, by the way, did anyone figure out if they were foam or ceramic?

We had fun the rest of the evening, but the pastry mishap weighed heavily on us. We didn't sleep well that night. The next morning my friend David insisted that we go back and confess. I agreed. We needed to apologize and pay for the damages. Ron and my brother had already gone to do something else, so David and I were left to face the consequences.

When we got back to the shop, we couldn't believe what we saw. There was the little baker, still smiling, still bobbing his head back and forth, and still moving his two trays up and down. But now the pastries were firmly wired on so they wouldn't fall off! Our damage had been minimal, but the effects were visible.

We went up to the counter to tell our story and accept the blame. I told the man at the cash register how we had been there the night before, and how it was crowded, and how we were admiring the little baker, and how one of us had knocked it over. We assumed that it had broken, and we were wrong in leaving, but we had come back to apologize and to pay for the damages. The man smiled. He seemed genuinely entertained. "You say you knocked it over?"

"Yes," we repeated.

"Which time?" he asked.

"I really don't know what time it was," I said. "Some time in the evening . . ." I started to calculate: before ten? after eight-thirty?

"No, I mean which time did you think you knocked him over: the first time? the second time? the third time? the fourth time?"

I was a little confused. I didn't know what he was talking about.

"He gets knocked over all the time," he said. "It's really not a good place for him. People are always bumping the counter. But when I move him back on the shelf, the customers ask for him. They like him. So I keep him up front. You can't really break him. He's made of metal. He gets bent out of shape, but we just bend him back."

"So he didn't really break?"

"Nah! But it was nice of you to come back anyway. Real nice. Thanks for trying to make it right."

David wanted a clarification before we left. "So the little baker is made out of metal, right?" He was smiling at me. We never considered metal. Ron and I were locked on ceramic, and the Davids were sure it was foam. We never thought of metal!

"Yeah. Metal. Except for the pastries on the tray. They're some kind of foam."

David smiled. Foam pastries. The Davids were right all along.

But did he rub it in? Not at all. We celebrated our friendship with cappuccino and some real Italian pastries.

Scripture

Matthew tells us that Jesus spoke these words to a crowd:

> So when you are offering your gift at the altar, if you remember that your brother or sister has something against you, leave your gift there before the altar and go; first be reconciled to your brother or sister, and then come and offer your gift.
>
> (5:23–24, NRSV)

Reflections

It's so important to right your wrongs. It's so important to reconcile.

What we did in the pastry shop wasn't as bad as we thought it was. But it was something we should have owned up to immediately. Instead, we chose to leave without doing so. That was wrong. But with every wrong, you always have another chance to do right.

So even when we mess up and do the wrong thing, we can still admit we were wrong, and then right the wrong. No use in doing wrong twice! or three times! or more!

Besides, there's nothing like being guilty to make you feel bad. And there's nothing like righting a wrong to make you feel good—except maybe an Italian pastry.

Did you ever do something wrong and then run away and not own up to it? How did that feel? Did you eventually right that wrong?

If you finally did right it, how long did it take? What was that like?

If you never did, why not? Is it really too late? Can you tell or apologize to anyone?

Has anyone ever done anything wrong to you and not apologized for it? If so, how do you feel about that person? Are you still friends? Have you had trouble with that relationship ever since?

What could right that wrong? What could heal your friendship? If your friend won't make the first move, can you?

Who Lost That Basketball Game?

Works Life

I was watching a junior high basketball game one afternoon. The teams seemed to be evenly matched, and the score was close.

Behind me several girls were talking about their friends, trying on each other's lipstick, paging through fashion magazines, and complaining about classes. They appeared to be paying little attention to the game, but they didn't seem to miss a play. Every time someone made a shot, they would praise the boy who made it. Every time they disagreed with the referee, they would express their disappointment. But they took it all very lightly. After all, this was just a game, right?

On the court it was serious basketball. An interesting dynamic was developing; the home team wasn't performing up to its potential. Three guys in particular seemed more determined to be stars than to be members of a team. They were throwing the ball away, attempting shots they couldn't make, and hogging the ball when other capable players were in position and open.

On the other hand, Eric was doing what good ballplayers do. He passed the ball when someone else was open, and he made most of the shots he attempted. It was clear he was a team player.

The score stayed close, and the girls continued to chat. At the end of the game, the home team was down by one point, but Eric was fouled. He would have to attempt two foul shots, knowing that his two points could win the game. Talk about pressure!

Eric was a good player, but he was shaking. He missed both shots, and the game was over. The three show-offs immediately began to criticize him and complain about how he lost the game and let the team down. I could tell he was devastated.

At the time, Eric didn't have the insight to realize that the other boys were the ones who had let the team down. By not being team players and by trying to act like superstars, they wasted many opportunities for the team to score. If they had played the way Eric played, his foul shots wouldn't have made any difference, because they would have already won the game.

How did the girls react? In my opinion they were the only ones who saw the truth. As they were collecting their things, one of them said, "Oh, well. Eric had a good day." Another commented casually, "Yeah, too bad those three jerks had to lose the game for us."

Scripture

The Gospels tell us about a time when a great argument broke out among the disciples about which one of them was the greatest. Jesus heard the loud talking, and he asked them what they were arguing about, but they didn't want to tell him. They were probably embarrassed.

Jesus already knew the topic of their conversation. He sat down with them to teach them an important lesson. He said that whoever wants to be the greatest has to learn to be the servant of others. The one who becomes the lowliest is the one who actually is the greatest. (This short story has different variations in three of the Gospels. You can find it in Matthew 18:1–4, Mark 9:33–35, and Luke 9:46–48.)

The three show-offs were each trying to be the greatest, looking out only for themselves. They ended up looking like jerks.

Eric was trying to be the servant. He tried to help every team member perform well. That's why he was the greatest.

The girls watching the game could see the difference clearly. It's a shame the boys didn't have the same insight.

Reflections

Have you ever tried to be "the greatest"? Did it work? What happened?

Were people impressed with who you were, or did they just notice how you were impressed with yourself?

Have you ever tried to be the servant? How did that work? Were you appreciated? Did you end up feeling lowly, or did you actually feel great?

The Lost Ring

I should have listened to Father Bryan.

I travel a lot. One hot day in September, I did a workshop in Alliance, Nebraska. It had been in the nineties, but by evening it was becoming cooler and more windy. In fact, Father Bryan said it would snow.

Snow in September? Tonight? After the hot temperatures we endured this afternoon? Ridiculous!

I didn't believe him. I didn't even close my window or remove my things from the windowsill. Why should I? The bedroom still hadn't cooled off. I didn't even need a blanket yet.

But the next morning, I awoke shivering. Snow covered the ground outside, and my things were almost frozen. I could hardly squeeze out my toothpaste, and my shampoo was as thick as molasses. When I saw him at breakfast, Father Bryan was already grinning. "I told you so," he smirked.

Later that day I was typing on my laptop computer when I glanced down at my hand and noticed my wedding ring was missing! I went running upstairs to tell everyone. We shook out the sheets and towels, retraced every possible step, and combed every inch of the carpet, but we could find nothing.

Somehow Father Bryan never gave up hope. "I know you will find your ring," he insisted. "Trust me. Remember the snow? You didn't believe me, but I was right, wasn't I? You see, I have a sense about these things." He grinned again.

I grinned back. But I was sure it was lost forever. I said the traditional Saint Anthony prayer (Tony, Tony, come on down. Something's lost and can't be found!), but I expected no miracles. I thought it must have gone down the drain while I was taking my shower. I called my husband, Ralph, and he consoled me over the phone.

Well, my travel week went on. Every day I visited a different parish in western Nebraska. My toothpaste ran out in Bridgeport, my skin lotion ran out in Scottsbluff, and my shampoo ran out in Sidney. In fact, in Sidney I threw out the empty shampoo bottle. But then I went back to retrieve it. I always tell my two sons not to throw away those little shampoo bottles—they are very handy, and you can always refill them.

By the time I was in North Platte, I had lost all hope. And to make matters worse, I had forgotten to buy new shampoo. Remembering the bottle I had rescued from the trash, I opened it up to see if I had enough left for just one more shower. As I looked inside, I couldn't believe what I saw! *My wedding ring was in it!*

Suddenly, it all made sense! It was so cold that morning in Alliance that my shampoo wouldn't come out of the bottle. I had to stick my ring finger into it to dig out some of that stubborn, thick mass the shampoo had hardened into. Evidently, the neck of the bottle had surrounded my wedding ring, and when I pulled my finger out, the ring slipped off, and I never felt a thing. The ring had been inside that shampoo bottle all along. I had actually thrown it out when I was in Sidney! If I hadn't gone back for the bottle, I never would have known what had happened to it.

I was so excited, I called up every person I had spent time with all week and shrieked with joy: "I found it! I found my ring!" Even people who didn't know I had lost my ring were getting phone calls from me. I still can't believe it happened.

A person could learn a lot from all this. Never shower with rings on. Always pray to Saint Anthony when you lose something. Don't throw away those little shampoo bottles. What did I learn? Listen to Father Bryan.

Scripture

Faith Fits Jesus tells a story about a woman who has ten silver coins, but she loses one of them. She lights a lamp and sweeps her whole house, frantically searching everywhere until she finds that missing coin. And when she finally finds it, she is so excited and happy that she invites all her friends and neighbors to her home and throws a big party to celebrate. (Luke 15:8–10)

Jesus says that God is like that woman. Just as she searches for a lost coin and celebrates when she finds it, God searches for our heart—especially when we have sinned. Anytime we repent of our sin, anytime we apologize or try to make right the wrong we have done, God celebrates and rejoices.

Reflections

When was the last time you lost something valuable? What happened? Did you ever find it? If so, how did you feel? If you felt joy and happiness, then that must be how God feels after finding us when we have gotten lost.

Home Sweet Home

Following is a note that was written on a card I received in October of my first year of college, from my best friend, Bob. Our two schools had their breaks scheduled on different weekends. He had come back home for his long weekend while I stayed at school.

> My dear Lisa,
> Just a quick note.
>
> I awoke this afternoon to an empty house. We arrived in New Jersey this morning after an all-night drive from Indiana. Now that I am home and settled, more than anything in the world, I want to dial 555-4425 and sit and chat for a few hours.
>
> "Home" always takes on a special meaning when one lives at college, but somehow it isn't really home without you.
> Love always,
> Bob

Home is often seen as a physical place. Home is where I live, my space, the place where I am comfortable, where my "stuff" is, my turf.

But essential to home is the people I love the most. If I had to choose between being in the place I call home or being with the people I love the most, I would probably choose the people. Because people are more important than places. We could probably pick up and move on and create a new home. It sure would be more difficult to pick ourselves up and create new loved ones.

Scripture

The Bible has lots of stories about people who had to move and leave their home. The following are two of them:

In the twelfth chapter of Genesis, God tells Abram to leave Haran, his homeland, with his wife, Sarai, and his nephew Lot, and to travel to a new land called Canaan. There Abram will father an entire people, with as many descendants as the stars in the sky. They get up and go! Abram trusts that God will provide for him.

In the second chapter of Matthew, an angel appears to Joseph in a dream and tells him to take his wife, Mary, and their new baby, Jesus, and to go immediately to Egypt in order to escape violence from Herod, who is seeking to kill their child. They get up and go! They trust that God will provide for them.

No matter what the urgency for moving is—a new job, a new climate, a new responsibility—it is still hard to move on. No matter what kind of transportation is available, it is still a lot of work, a lot of disruption. It takes faith to trust that God will provide for us when we find it necessary to move and make a new home.

Reflections

Did you ever move? What was it like? What was the best or worst part of moving?

What is your home like? What is your room like? If you had to change rooms, or change homes, or move to a new state or country, what would you hope to have in your new home? What would you miss the most? What might ease the pain of having to move?

Because of Your Youth

When my son Michael was in junior high, he had a summer job detasseling corn. He would get on a bus early in the morning, when it was still dark outside, and ride to designated cornfields where they were growing hybrid corn. His job was to walk up and down certain rows of corn, pulling off the tassels so the corn would breed correctly. It was hard work. Mornings were often cold and wet and muddy; afternoons hot and dry and dusty. If the bugs and sunburn didn't make him miserable, the corn rash did. Every day he came home filthy, hot, and exhausted.

He saved his hard-earned money and bought a mountain bike. He had been looking around for a while, and he knew just what he wanted. When he and his dad brought it home, he couldn't wait to ride it. He got on it and took off. He was only partway down the block when the bike practically fell apart right under him. He lost control and crashed. He walked the bike back to the house. It was clear that he had been sold a bike that wasn't assembled properly. Loose screws came out, parts separated, and it crumpled during the ride.

He brought it back to the shop, told his story, and was promised a brand-new bike. He waited and waited, and called the place for weeks. When his "new" bike finally came in, he went to pick it up. Upon arriving home with it, he noticed something strange. This was not a new bike at all. It was his old bike—which they had "fixed up." But Michael could still find the same scratches he recognized from his crash, and the dents that were pounded out and repainted. He was promised a new bike, not the same one patched up. He felt cheated and tricked. And he thought they had tried to take advantage of him because he was a young teenager. He didn't think they would have treated an adult that way.

At first he was angry. He didn't want his dad to go in and "straighten things out" for him. So he thought he had no choice but to accept this bicycle.

But then he decided to write a letter. We don't have a copy of it anymore, but it was very simple. He told the facts of the story. He said he was given a bike that wasn't ready to be ridden, he had crashed, and then he had been promised a brand-new bike. What he had received was the old one, patched up and repainted. He said that he had been taught to always tell the truth, and that he had trusted this bike shop and didn't understand why they had done what they did. He asked for an explanation.

Not long after that, he got a phone call and an apology, and another promise for a brand-new bicycle, which he did receive. Every screw was tight, and he never had any trouble with it.

When his bike crashed, Michael had several options. He could have acted nasty, he could have given up, he could have sought revenge, but he did none of these immature things. He was honest and upfront, and he told his story. He was polite, but he wanted what he had been promised. And he got it.

He was a good example of how all young people need to act when they think they are not being treated fairly. And he got results.

Scripture

Do not let anyone look down on you because you are young, but be an example for the believers in your speech, your conduct, your love, faith, and purity. (1 Timothy 4:12, GNB)

Timothy was a young Christian who became Paul's assistant in his missionary work. Obviously, it was not always easy for Timothy to be a leader. Young people are not always treated with the same respect as older people. Yet Paul told him not to be discouraged, to do the right thing, behave well, and let his example speak for itself. It worked for Timothy. It worked for Michael. It can work for you.

Reflections

Do you ever feel looked down upon because of your youth? In a store or a restaurant, do you think you are given the same respect and service that an older person would get? Why or why not? What usually happens?

Do you have any teachers who respect you and listen to you, who know you as an individual and value you as a person? What is that like? How do they show their attitude?

Do you always show respect to all your teachers, to your parents, and to all adults you encounter? Why or why not? How do you usually act? What results does that behavior bring? What attitude do your actions show?

Lovesick Teenage Blues

Part One

I recently met you.
I like you a lot.
But I'm not going to think about you. No, I'm not.

I'm not going to wonder and worry like this:
Will we ever hold hands?
Will we cuddle and kiss?
Will you laugh at my jokes?
Will you like what I wear?
Will you scratch my back?
Will you play with my hair?

No. This time I'm smooth.
I've got it down pat.
I'm not going to wonder and worry like that.
I'm not going to care if you like me or not.

You're just a new friend.
I just like you.
A lot.

Part Two

You like me!
You kissed me!
A blessing!
A curse!
I thought it was better!
But no! Now it's worse!

You said you would call me.
But what if you don't?
I think this could work out.
But what if it won't?

You told me your birthday.
Should I get you a card?
Should I get you a present?
Deciding is hard!

Should I tell my mother?
Should I tell my best friend?
Is this a new start?
Or will this soon end?
Are we now a "couple"?
Or is this just a fling?
I'm just so confused about everything!

It was better pretending that I didn't care.
It was easy to think of the things we don't share.

But now that you kissed me
(And I kissed you, too!),
Everything's different!
So what should I do?

Part Three

You said you would call me.
But you didn't call.
I waited and waited.
You still didn't call.

I started to wonder: Are you all right?
Did you forget?
Where are you tonight?
Do you still like me?
I really feel blue.
Two times in a row it was I who called you!

So now it's your turn.
I'll just have to wait.
I'll sit at this phone
Until it gets late.

Well, later and later and later it got.
You said you would call me.
But no, you did not!

I waited and waited,
Then finally called you.
How stupid I was!
What a dumb thing to do!

You were asleep!
You weren't gonna call!
You didn't remember to call me at all!

We talked for a bit.
You tried to be nice.
But you were so tired, you yawned at me twice!

Oh, why did I call you?
Why couldn't I wait?
By the time I decided to call, it was late!

How stupid I was!
What a dumb thing to do!
Three times in a row now,
I have called you!

One thing for sure,
Next time I'll wait.
I won't call you next time,
No matter how late.
I have it all planned.
I've got it down pat.
Next time and next time and the time after that.
'Til four times go by and it's you who's called me!
That's how I want this new friendship to be!

'Cuz that way I'll know
You still like me and all.
So then I won't care
The next time you don't call.

Part Four

It finally happened!
We had our first fight!
I tossed and I turned and I grumbled all night!

Why did I say it?
I feel like a jerk!
Oh, I should have known that this could not work!

We started off great!
We kissed and held hands!

You wanted to see me, and so we made plans.
You gave me a call.
You sent me a note.
You wrote and you called!
You called and you wrote!
You told me you liked me.
You kissed me.
A lot!
But now things are different,
Like it or not.

You say you are busy.
You have lots to do.
Too busy to see me? Well, I'm busy, too!

I'm that unimportant? I guess I don't rate!
Or else you'd find time, you'd make time, for a date!
I said, "You don't care!" and "I'm not going to chase
    you!"
But now I'm embarrassed.
Oh, how can I face you?
You called me "demanding."
You "needed your space."
Well, now you can spread out all over the place!
And if you think I'm gonna crawl back, well, I'm not!

I don't even like you.
Not even a lot.

Part Five

What's this in the mail?
Did you send me a note?
It's been a whole week since the last time you wrote!
How come you are writing?
I thought you didn't care.
I thought you were busy with no time to spare!

Shall I open your letter?
Shall I see what you wrote?
You know I'm so busy, no time for a note!
Well, maybe this once, I'll see what you say.
I could use a good laugh. I've had a hard day.

What's this?
"I am sorry."
You're sorry, you say?
And you feel bad about what you said yesterday?
And you say you will call me?
I've heard that before.
I *don't* want to wait for your calls anymore.
In fact, I was leaving.
To do many things.
I won't even be *here* when that telephone rings!

Oh, no! The phone's ringing!
I hope it's not you!
What should I say?
What should I do?
I just won't answer.
I'm ready to go.
But then if it's you, I won't even know.
Should I pick up the phone?
As long as I'm cool . . .
I really don't like you . . .
I won't be a fool.

"Hello"
(Oh my gosh! It really is you!)
"I just got your card."
"Yes, I'm sorry, too."

Part Six

O wonderful world! O planet divine!
Every sweet pleasure on earth can be mine!
The sun is a masterpiece, rising at dawn!
The rains come down gently, refreshing the lawn!
Life is so beautiful! Thank God above!
Once again, I am madly in love!

It started out slowly.
We met just by chance!
But I saw the love behind every shy glance!
Not once did I question your love from the start!
I never had reason to doubt your true heart!

Did I bring up the fact that your beautiful eyes
Have more sparkle in them than the stars in the skies?
Did I happen to mention your sweet, dreamy voice
That calls me to love you? I don't have a choice!
Did it ever come up that your smile's so bright
That I can see heaven in the darkest of night?

Yes, there are some lovers—unlucky, I'm told—
Who end up with sweethearts too careless or bold,
Who can't find the time to make time for a date,
And cause broken hearts to cry, worry, and wait;
Who say they will call, but then promptly forget!
But, oh! Such a person I never have met!

No, my honey's not like that!
Thank heaven above!
Or else I would never have fallen in love!

Part Seven

Why does this happen, again and again?
You finally said it: "Let's just be friends."

What must I do in order to find
A person who won't drive me out of my mind?

Why did you have to play games and pretend?
Why lead me on, if this is the end?
Are you scared of commitment? Scared of the truth?
Scared you're not wild enough for your youth?
Why change your mind about me every day?
Why draw me closer, then push me away?

Oh, give me a sweetie who knows how to give,
Knows how to be honest, knows how to live,
Who's brave enough to admit being scared,
Who's grown-up enough to respect what is shared!

Until I can find such a lover and friend,
I'll have to risk going through all this—*again!*

Scripture

Faith
Fits

The Book of Sirach says, "No wound is as serious as wounded love" (Sirach 25:13, GNB).

People in romantic relationships have been mis-understanding each other for centuries! It's nothing new. Each person is different, and yet wants to be in relation-ship with another. So relating is quite a struggle. Some-times it seems as if everything is wonderful, and you've found the perfect boyfriend or girlfriend. Other times you may wonder how you ever saw anything good about that "jerk" who just broke up with you!

Reflections

What's the best part about romance? What's the worst part?

What kind of person are you looking for? Is it usually difficult to find such a person? Why or why not? As you get older, do you think it will become harder or easier? Why?

Your "success" in romantic relationships is often related to your success with friendship in general.

What are your relationships like with friends of your same gender? What are your relationships like with friends of the other gender? Is it harder for you to understand your friends of the other gender or of the same gender?

The Last Shall Be First

During my last two years of college, I was on the Holy Cross varsity swim team. Now don't get excited and think that I was a jock. Let me explain. I only swam one event regularly—the 50-Free—fifty yards freestyle. Down and back. Two pool lengths. And typically I would dive in and swim the first length without even breathing, putting everything I had into that swim. I would do my turn, come up for air, look around the pool, and then notice that I was the only one still swimming. Everyone else had already finished the race!

If I was that slow, how did I manage to make the team? Well, they had twenty slots for swimmers, and I was number twenty! There wasn't anyone better trying to get on the team. There wasn't anyone else at all! So there I was.

However, let me tell you about my finest hour.

Half the team was out sick, and we were trying to figure out how to beat this one team, or at least to tie the meet. Our coach had figured out that our top three swimmers would have to get first place in each of their events. That meant that one of the swimmers would have to swim two events in a row: the 500-yard freestyle— twenty pool lengths—a real killer; and then the 200-yard butterfly, another real killer.

Understandably, Rita, the person chosen to swim the two events, was a bit stressed. She argued with the coach: "Which one do you want me to go all out on? I can't win both!" He argued back, "You've got to win both!" Rita insisted, "I can't win both!" The coach scrunched up his face and thought.

Suddenly, a strange and eerie grin slid across his face. "Lisa," he called to me, "go find out if the exhibition lane is free for that 500-yard freestyle event." I asked. Yes, it was free. I told the coach. (The exhibition lane is the leftover lane that doesn't belong to either team in the meet. Swimmers from either team can sign up to swim unofficially under meet conditions to see what their time would be. Coaches often use that lane to try out a swimmer in a new stroke. If a swimmer in that lane beats everyone else in the race, that swimmer still doesn't win the event. Swimming there doesn't count.)

The coach looked at me and said, "Then you are swimming the five hundred."

I was shocked. "Me? Why me?" Recall that everyone swims approximately twice as fast as I do, meaning that I would be swimming ten of the twenty pool lengths alone, not exactly something to look forward to.

Then the eerie grin returned to his face. "By the time you finish that race, Rita will have plenty of time to rest."

Get it? He asked me because I was the slowest!

By the way, we didn't win that meet—but we tied.

Scripture

Jesus said, "Thus, the last will be first, and the first will be last" (Matthew 20:16, NAB).

According to Jesus, if we were all content to be last, we'd all be first. We'd all be on the winning team. And we wouldn't even have a losing team. That's an image of heaven I can relate to.

Reflections

When in life have you felt like a winner? Were you ever on a team that won a game or a tournament? Did you ever win a contest? Did you think you were better than the ones who lost? Is anyone ever really "better" than someone else? What makes a person a real winner?

Washing Feet
and Clipping Toenails

While I was in high school, my grandfather lived with us for a while. He was too old to live by himself. My mother usually took care of his needs, but one day she asked me to clip his toenails.

What I said to her was, "Okay." But what I thought inside my mind was, "Clip Grandpa's toenails? *Clip Grandpa's toenails!!??* I've never done that before! How do you clip someone else's toenails?"

Maybe she thought I had watched her do it. Maybe she thought I had actually done it before. Maybe she was mixing me up with one of my brothers who might have done it before.

Anyway, I was in the living room with the toenail clippers, and Grandpa was sitting on the couch.

"Mom says you would like me to clip your toenails, Grandpa. Can I do that for you now?"

What he said to me was, "Okay. Sure."

But I wonder what he thought inside his mind. "She never did this before! Why is she the one doing this? Is she going to miss and hurt me? Will she do a good job? Whose idea was this anyway?"

So I helped him get his slippers off. His feet were like, well, they were like old mans' feet: not perfectly clean, and a little smelly.

But it really wasn't a big deal. It didn't take very long. It wasn't really difficult. And as I did it, I realized that it was something he really couldn't do himself. So it was good that I was there to help him. And I did worry that maybe he wouldn't like the way I did it.

When it was done, I simply said, "Okay. All done now."

He simply said, "Good girl."

I cleaned up, and that was that.

I don't think I ever mentioned it to my mom, and she never asked me about it. I don't think I ever mentioned it to anyone. But I thought about it for the rest of the day. And for the rest of the week.

Kneeling down and working on someone's feet. Not very glamorous. Not something you brag about or tell your friends about. But somehow I felt important that day.

Scripture

Faith
Fits

The day before he died, Jesus was having supper for the last time with his friends and Apostles.

At one point he stood up from the table, took off his outer garment, wrapped a towel around his waist, and knelt at the feet of his followers. With a basin and pitcher, he washed and dried their feet.

> This was the work of a servant. But Jesus the Christ, the Anointed One, the Messiah, Almighty God in a human body, knelt before his disciples, and taught them to be servants for each other and for the world. (Adapted from John 13:12–15, GNB)

Reflections

When have others served you and taken care of your needs? When have you taken care of the needs of someone else?

Have you ever changed a baby's diaper or cleaned up after a sick child? Have you ever cooked or cleaned for an older family member or a neighbor?

Most of us learn how to serve the needs of others by living in a family and watching how people who love one another take care of one another.

What are examples of this from your family?

They Will Hold You Up

I have a beautiful goddaughter named Bernadette. She lives in the house where I grew up, which is in New Jersey. Now I live in the Midwest, but I try to visit her as often as I can.

Whenever I visit, I stay in the room that used to be my room as a teenager. It's just six steps up from Bernadette's room. The stairs turn a corner, and they form a wonderful place for sitting. So it's a place where Bernadette and I often play together. We line up stuffed animals or cups and saucers or dolls on every step.

One afternoon Bernadette and I were playing there. She was three years old at the time. The front door opened and shut, and a familiar voice said, "Hello?" Bernadette said, "Uncle David!" and we both started to come down the steps as my brother David came up the steps. We met in the middle for hugs. Bernadette showed him the toys we had been playing with. Then we sat on the floor and talked and played for a while.

When Bernadette came down the steps to fetch more toys, she tripped and began to fall. She had about three steps left, and she was falling through the air, head-first, toward the floor.

I remember sitting there, thinking: "How slowly she seems to be falling. I'll just reach up and catch her gently so she doesn't hurt herself." I caught her and held her and effortlessly brought her to the floor. The whole incident happened in silence and without any struggle or difficulty. Once she was back on the floor and safe, she realized what had happened, and she started to cry. In no time at all, Heidi, Bernadette's mom and my sister-in-law, came running up the steps. We assured her that Bernadette wasn't hurt, only scared. Heidi asked, "What happened?"

David said: "Bernadette tripped, and before I could even move, Lisa had jumped up and snatched her, right before she hit the floor! She moved like lightning! I never saw anyone move so fast!"

I was surprised. I told them both that I had felt as if the world were in slow motion. It seemed so easy for me to just lean over and catch her.

Later, my brother Joe, Bernadette's dad, came home. Bernadette told him what had happened on the steps. In reply, Joe told us a similar story. One day he was carrying Bernadette as he walked through a store parking lot in the rain. He tripped and began to fall forward. As he was falling forward, he realized that he had to protect Bernadette, who was about to be smashed into the pavement and then crushed by his body on top of hers. So as the world moved in slow motion, he was able to lift her way up over his head so that he would hit the ground but she wouldn't.

He was successful. He cut his face and arms, and his shirt was all ripped. But Bernadette was safe.

When we have to protect someone, how does everything switch to slow motion? How are we able to do things that normally seem to be impossible?

Scripture

God will put . . . angels in charge of you
    to protect you wherever you go.
They will hold you up with their hands
    to keep you from hurting your feet on the
      stones.

(Psalm 91:11–12, GNB)

Do I believe that angels intervene and protect us? I guess it's possible. I also believe that when we care about someone who is in danger, we are suddenly capable of doing things we could never accomplish on our own. Scientists would call it adrenaline. Romantics would call it courage. Perhaps we are called to be the angels the psalmist talks about.

Reflections

Have you ever had to respond in an emergency? Did you ever do something brave without thinking about it? What was that like?

In emergencies, do you experience strength that you don't normally have? Have you ever considered yourself to be an angel for others?

Signing Yearbooks

The following are excerpts from the notes my three best friends wrote in my yearbook, the year we graduated from Union Catholic High School:

From Bob:

Dear Lisa, I hate to grasp at clichés when even the grasping has become a cliché. You know it's inadequate to say words like "There are no words . . ." or "We've come a long way . . ." I'm not quite as meticulous as you, and did not write a first draft. So forgive my rambling.

Let me begin by saying there are no words and we've come a long way . . .

I tried to explain to you the other night how much of a friend you are to me and how much I need you and love you . . .

From Frances:

It seems especially reminiscent for me to sign this yearbook tonight. Tomorrow I am starting college. God, the time flew past. This summer is like a blur —yet I will always remember it as a time when we enjoyed the type of loving friendship that comes too few times in a lifetime. Thank you for everything. I mean it, every little thing. I'm here whenever you need me. And know that I wish to continue our friendship for years to come. We have something great. Please, let's not let time, space, and differences destroy it.

From Mike:

In the past year and a half, you have been a tremendous help to me in growing up. We've shared a lot of love, laughs, and tears. Love, which has made a definite impression in my heart; laughs, which enabled both of us to forget our troubles and enjoy life; and tears, which can only be a sign that we are human—real, live, loving, mature people—because only this type of person can cry for a cause. Friendships such as ours help us to live through the trying times and to enjoy the many gifts we do have . . .

And years from now, when you look at my picture, try not to laugh too hard when you remember, "Oh, this is the creep I went to my junior prom with!"

All of us pledged to stay true to one another and to be friends for life. Did we stay friends? Sort of. We kept in close touch for a long time. But of course, we moved on with our lives. And when we did connect again, it was special. These are the three people that were with me when I began to understand what life was really all about. They know me in a way very few people do.

We had our twentieth high school reunion not too long ago. I was excited to go, and excited to see everyone again. Almost a year ahead of time, I started to get in touch with everyone again. It was great fun: letters and phone calls and arrangements to visit with one another the summer before the reunion.

Frances and I both have teenage sons now. It was fun to get together and share the joys and challenges of being a teenager today as well as twenty years ago. She and I are still similar in many ways.

Mike and I still can't stop laughing whenever we are together. I don't know who usually starts it, but it's contagious. Pretty soon everything is funny, even things that make no sense, and I remember how much I loved being with him.

It was more difficult to reconnect with Bob. I had continued to write to him over the years, but in the last two or three years, I had not received any replies. Even the Christmas cards stopped coming. I knew that once we were back together, it would seem like "old times" again, so I wasn't overly concerned. Until I was told that he had passed away almost a year earlier. No wonder my last Christmas card was sent back marked "address unknown."

Mike had tried to contact me, but after several unsuccessful attempts, he had given up.

So we went to our reunion, the three of us instead of the four of us. It began with a Mass at Union Catholic High School in memory of Bob and the other classmates of ours who had died.

Friendship is a precious thing.

Scripture

A loyal friend is like a safe shelter; find one, and you have found a treasure. Nothing else is as valuable; there is no way of putting a price on it. A loyal friend is like a medicine that keeps you in good health.

(Sirach 6:14–16, GNB)

Reflections

Who are your close friends? What do you like about them? What do they like about you?

Have you lost a good friend, either through death or by just losing contact? How have you dealt with it?

Have you ever had a fight with a friend that ruined your friendship? Can you think of any way that you can make up again and renew your friendship?

As You Fly the Friendly Skies

I used to live in a small town in central Nebraska. The airport serviced only small commuter planes, the kind with less than twenty seats. It's nice because every seat is both an aisle seat and a window seat. But it's not so nice when you're flying through some rough air, because you feel every bump and bounce.

Well, I was flying to Denver on one of those little planes, and the weather was turbulent. We were getting slammed back and forth all over the plane, and I'm sure I heard someone in the back filling up one of those air sickness bags that they have in every seat pocket.

The woman across the aisle from me was elderly, and I wondered how she was taking all this jolting and roller-coaster riding. But every time I looked at her, she was smiling and looking very content. I wondered if she could really feel as comfortable as she looked.

When the flight was over, I had to take a van to a different terminal to catch the next flight. This same woman ended up sitting across from me again. I asked her, "How did you like that flight we were on?"

She just smiled and said, "Oh, I just made up my mind to enjoy the flight, and so I did."

"What's your secret?"

She leaned over and whispered, "Do you really want to know?"

I nodded.

"I pray."

I couldn't believe my ears. Was she for real? She continued: "First I pray for the pilot. Then I pray for each person in the plane. Then I look on the ground, and I find a car. I follow that car with my eyes until I can't see it anymore, and I pray for whoever is in that car. Then I find another car. When we're so high up in the clouds that I can't see any more cars, I think of my family—my children and grandchildren—and I pray for each one of them. Then, when I run out of family members, I come back to the people in the plane, and I start looking down the aisle and praying for each one of them again. This keeps me pretty occupied. I get to feeling so thankful, I don't have room in my heart to be concerned with turbulence."

I just sat in silence. I was in shock. Here I was worrying about her condition, and she was praying for me! "You always do this?" I asked her.

"I don't fly very often. Just to visit my grandchildren. I have some on the East Coast and some on the West Coast. But the praying is my daughter's idea. I think it's a dandy. Now all of us in the family do it whenever we fly."

This woman's whole family prays for people in cars that they see from airplanes. And now I do it, too. I've told this story to people all over the country, and I know many of them do it now, as well. And every time I see a plane above me, I wonder if someone up there is praying for us folks down below. I make it a point to look up and pray for the folks in that plane, too, whoever they are.

Scripture

Hear my cry, O God;
      listen to my prayer!
In despair and far from home,
      I call to you.

Take me to a safe refuge,

. . . .
      let me find safety under your wings

. . . .
I will always sing praises to you.

(Psalm 61:1–8, GNB)

Reflections

Do you ever think that some stranger has prayed for you? Do you pray to God to help you when you are worried or afraid? Do you pray for people you love? Do you pray for strangers?

Who Would Have Thought?

Now it's time for a lesson in ancient Greek. My dad used to have this phrase that he would repeat every time something unusual happened. He would even write it down for you. This is how it looks:

$$Τισ \ ανωεθαι \ ταυτα \ γενεστι$$

This is how it sounds:

Tis on-away-thay tau-tah ga-nes-ti.
(In *tau-tah*, the "tau" rhymes with "how.")

This phrase may seem like a strange thing to say, but our family was raised to say it. Any coincidence, any situation that was somehow ironic, unusual, or surprising, was a fitting occasion for this phrase. When other families might be saying to one another, "Wow! How strange! What a coincidence!" our family would say, "Tis on-away-thay tau-tah ga-nes-ti," which means, "Who would have ever thought that this could have happened?"

Not only was this a phrase that one of us could say to another, but it could be done in a choral method, a method used whereby one family member would say, "Tis on-away-thay," and another family member (or the rest of the family) would answer, "Tau-tah ga-nes-ti."

You may find this hard to believe, but I have taught this little phrase to a few groups of people. There are actually some young adults walking around who learned this as teenagers; and even today I can say to them, "Tis on-away-thay," and they will respond with, "Tau-tah ga-nes-ti." And it's not just a "teenager" thing. I have taught this to adults as well. Some of them have even asked for a copy of the words written in Greek.

Please understand. My dad was not an ancient Greek expert. In fact, he would have been the first to admit to you that this was almost the only thing he could remember from his entire Greek course. And if you copy down those Greek letters and memorize how to pronounce the phrase and write it, you will then know almost as much Greek as he knew.

So why would you do such a thing? Well, why not? Someday, somewhere, when you least expect it, someone may come up to you and utter those fateful words, "Tis on-away-thay." And not only will you be able to answer correctly, "Tau-tah gan-es-ti," but you will also be able to actually write it down in Greek! Now that would be a coincidence!

And who would have ever thought that this could have happened?

Scripture

Faith
Fits
What no one ever saw or heard,
what no one ever thought could happen,
is the very thing God prepared for those
who love . . .

(1 Corinthians 2:9, GNB)

Reflections

In the quote from the Scriptures, Paul is talking about heaven. What God has prepared for us in heaven will be so spectacular, so awesome, that we never can imagine it. What heaven is like is something our eyes have never seen and our ears have never heard of—something we never can imagine. Just try to picture that. Try to imagine the unimaginable.

I know my dad is there waiting for me to come. And I know what we'll say to each other. He'll say, "Tis on-away-thay," and I'll answer, "Tau-tah gan-es-ti." "Who would have ever thought that this could have happened?"

What is your image of heaven? What would be the perfect existence? Will it be an existence that would prompt you to say, "Tis on-away-thay tau-tah gan-es-ti"? "Who would have ever thought that this could have happened?"

No Longer Black or White

During my second year of college, I roomed with a senior. We got along well, but she would be graduating, and I needed to find another roommate.

I really liked one girl in my acting class. Her name was Caroline. Whenever we rehearsed scenes together, I enjoyed her company. But I didn't know if she had a roommate for the next year. And I was afraid to ask—because she was black, and I am white.

I never knew of any roommate pairs that were racially mixed, and I was just too afraid to ask her. Maybe I thought she might be upset with me for asking. I don't know. But I never asked her.

I eventually did find a roommate. And things worked out fine. But I always wished that I had found the courage to ask Caroline. She was bright and fun, easy to get along with, and considerate—everything you would want a roommate to be.

The following year we were in another play together. I heard her talking to someone else about how frantic she had been the year before because she hadn't been able to find a roommate.

Later, after practice, I stopped her. "Caroline, did I hear you say that last year you were looking for a roommate?"

"Yes, I was," she answered.

"I wish I had known that."

"Why?" she asked.

"Because I needed a roommate, and I wanted to ask you. But I was afraid to ask you. I didn't know what you would have thought about rooming with a white person."

Her eyes grew wide. "I wanted to ask you, too. But I was afraid you might not want to room with a black person."

We looked at each other and fought back the tears as we realized what our fears had done to us. We hugged and then laughed, knowing how foolish we both had been.

Scripture

Faith
Fits

In Christ there is no Jew or Greek, slave or citizen, male or female. All are one in Christ Jesus.

(Galatians 3:28, INT)

In this passage from the Scriptures, Paul is protesting the separations and distinctions that his culture made among people.

Reflections

Do you have friends of another race? If so, do you talk about your racial differences and learn from one another? Or do you ignore them and pretend that the differences aren't there? If you don't have friends of another race, why not? Do you just not know anyone from a different racial heritage, or are you afraid to get too close to a person who may be so different from yourself?

Would you date someone of another race? Why or why not? If you were an adult, would you adopt a child of another race? What do you think is the biggest challenge for people of different races when it comes to respect and better relationships?

Crumbs
from the Rich Family's Table

Snow was falling fast and furious one day, and my two sons stayed home from school. One was in junior high then, and the other was just two grades behind him. My husband, Ralph, was still at work, but it was late in the afternoon, and we expected him home soon.

We heard a knock at the door. When I opened the door, a man with tattered, dirty clothing was standing there. I could smell an unpleasant odor that obviously belonged to him. He asked if he could shovel our driveway for some food. It seemed like a silly question to me because it was obvious that the driveway and sidewalks had already been cleared. Somehow he didn't seem to notice. So I told him that we didn't need him to do that for us; that it was already done. He didn't seem to understand what I was saying. I asked him if he would like some food anyway. He said yes. He asked specifically for coffee. I left him on the porch and went into our kitchen. By then Michael and Ralphie had joined me, and were caught up with the excitement of having a stranger visiting us. I was looking for items that he could eat either now or later, whichever he wanted. I had two individual fruit pies that we had bought recently at the store—the boys had asked me for them, and they had each picked one out. Ralphie spoke up, "You could give him my fruit pie." Michael was quick to join in, "You could give him mine, too." I thanked them for their generosity, and put the fruit pies into a bag. I made a couple of sandwiches while the coffee brewed. It felt strange to have him waiting on the porch, but he didn't seem to mind.

I stuck some napkins and some wet wipes into the bag. I poured the coffee into one of those big foam cups, and I brought it to him along with the bag of food. He asked me if he could use our bathroom. I was really uncomfortable with this, but I just couldn't seem to refuse. I told him it was upstairs, to the right. He put the bag and the coffee down on a bench on the porch and went upstairs. I kept the boys downstairs.

It seemed like a long time before he finally came downstairs. I was worried. I was thinking that I had done the wrong thing, and I was feeling very foolish. But then we heard the door open, and he came downstairs. He thanked us very much and went toward the front door. He picked up his bag and the cup of coffee, and we said, "Good-bye." He asked me if I had a husband, and if I needed one. He said he was very handy. I told him I had one, and he would be home any minute. He nodded. We never saw him again.

He had given us his name, and so I called one of the churches in town that had a well-developed outreach to the homeless, to ask if they had ever heard of him. No, they hadn't. I told them I had let him into the house to use the bathroom, and they told me that that wasn't a very smart thing to do. It would have been better to direct him to the closest gas station or church, or to the homeless shelter. They were probably right. We never forgot him, although now none of us seem to be able to remember his name.

Our next direct experience with feeding the hungry didn't come until many years later, when my two sons were both in high school. But I will let you read the words of my son Ralph, who not only wrote this up as an essay, but got it published in a family newsletter called "HomeWord."

> One night when I was eating supper, my father told our family that he had signed us up to work at the soup kitchen on December fifteenth. When I heard this, I got very mad at my parents. I told them that I was not going to help, no matter what. My parents wanted to know why I didn't want to help. At the time I couldn't describe my feelings. It did not matter. I had to go.
>
> When I first arrived at the soup kitchen, there seemed to be a lot of excitement. I had a very easy job. I had to lay out the bowls so the chili could be spooned into them.
>
> My mom did ask me if I wanted to go out where the people were and help collect the trash. I said okay.

I went out there, and my mom started to talk to the people. I had a really hard time trying to talk, so I went back to the serving bowls.

The reason I went back is because I did not know what to say to the people who were eating. I felt that we didn't have very much in common. I was afraid that if I said something "wrong," I might offend them or make them feel uncomfortable. I was also afraid that they might talk about their problems. If they did, there was nothing I could do or say to help them. It was just easier to focus on serving the food. It felt awkward.

I also felt very sorry for them. The worst part was when someone from my own school came in. I felt awfully bad for him and his family. We just said "hi" and went back to business.

I feel bad that a lot of people are so selfish. We don't have to be, and that is what makes me feel so ashamed. I felt so embarrassed because I have so much, and yet I still want more. It is very hard not to want more, so I do. I guess that makes me greedy. I have to have more when some people do not have any. I realized this when I saw the people at the soup kitchen.

As of right now, I feel different about helping the poor. I will help the next time I am asked. I will not be so unwilling. If everyone had the same attitude as I did in the beginning, then nothing would ever change. I am glad that my parents signed me up to help. They did the right thing, and they knew it. I am thankful that they made me go.

Scripture

Faith Fits Jesus tells a story about a rich man and a poor man. We know the poor man's name—Lazarus. But we aren't told the rich man's name.

The rich man seems to let Lazarus hang out near his home—by the gate. His dogs even lick Lazarus's open sores. How many of us would be comfortable with a homeless person living in our backyard?

And for all of this man's tolerance, when both of them die, the rich man doesn't go to heaven. He can see Lazarus in heaven from where he is, but the rich man is burning in the fire. (Luke 16:19–31)

Reflections

Do you ever think about people who are without food, without homes, without jobs? What can you or your family or your school or your parish do to become more involved with taking care of those in need?

Do you appreciate what you have? Or do you take it for granted? Do you really need everything you have? How many of your "needs" are actually luxuries?

What do you think of the attitude change that my son Ralph expressed in his essay?

Love Is . . .

Works Life

My very best friend in high school was Bob. We never dated. We were just really good friends. We discussed everything. Everything! Intensely! We really trusted each other, and we both loved to analyze our feelings and thoughts. We would have made great philosophers.

At one point during high school, I wrote this poem for him. I was very much into Shakespeare at the time, so I used words like *thee* and *thy* instead of *you* and *your*.

How can I my love for thee express?
If I would say, "I love thee very much,"
My words could capture not the tenderness
Our hands both feel, when mine and thine do touch.
And neither could the finest gift of gold
Upon engraved, "To Thee with all my love,"
Rest my mind in knowing I had told
Thee all th' emotions words might tell thee of.
Thou knowest all we share shall always be;
For no matter the many days we are apart,
Reminded not by sight nor voice of thee,
My love will still be thine, like all my heart.
The thought of thee forever I shall keep;
For never have I known a love so deep.

Our senior year we all were asked to choose a quotation to go under our graduation picture for the yearbook. Bob chose the last two lines of that poem to go under his picture. It was a surprise. I was very touched.

The following is an excerpt from a letter Bob wrote to me in February of our first year in college:

My day-to-day inconveniences still waste my time (a crooked smile, a lousy lunch, a failed test), but hopefully the lifelong inconsistencies are being ironed out. That's growing up. That is what college is for.

We need a delicate balance between day-to-day inconveniences and lifelong inconsistencies. We need perspective. Nothing matters except for love, and because of love, everything matters. Thank you for your love.

One of the things we loved to talk about was love and relationships, especially ours. We were always trying to explain how we felt about each other—how it seemed different from other relationships.

Love is like that. It baffles people. It's hard to describe. It's hard to define. But people keep trying.

Scripture

Love is patient; love is kind; love is not envious or boastful or arrogant or rude. It does not insist on its own way; it is not irritable or resentful; it does not rejoice in wrongdoing, but rejoices in the truth. It bears all things, believes all things, hopes all things, endures all things.

Love never ends.

(1 Corinthians 13:4–8, NRSV)

Reflections

Part of growing up is discovering what love is all about. Most of us experience love first from our parents and families. But learning about love "in the real world" is a whole different experience.

How would you define love? What do you think about the description of love from Paul's First Letter to the Corinthians?

Often a person is closer to a friend than he or she is to the person in a dating relationship. Sometimes, when friends start to date, it ruins their friendship. If they break up, they can't ever be "just friends" again. So some people believe that falling in love will just ruin their love or friendship. What do you think?

Let Me Go with You

At one time in my life, I lived in Alabama. I then was offered a job in Michigan. I had to move. It's quite a long drive from Alabama to Michigan, and I really didn't think I could manage it by myself.

My brother David offered to help me. We didn't have to load boxes into a truck by ourselves because the moving-van people took care of that. But getting everything organized and packed, then driving, and then getting everything unpacked and reorganized was quite a job.

Not only that, it was difficult emotionally for me to move. I didn't know anyone in Michigan. I would be starting a new job in a new place, and I lived alone. It was a little overwhelming, to say the least.

David came along and helped me with everything. And I'll be honest with you. I would like to tell you how much fun we had together. But we didn't have that much fun.

I wasn't easy to get along with in those days. It was a stressful time for me, and I wasn't very patient. I wasn't always nice to David. And I should have been because he was doing me such a huge favor. But somehow he understood. He was so good to me.

In fact, he didn't even have a definite time planned for his departure. He said that he would stay with me as long as I needed him. He would stay until I felt comfortable with everything and thought that I could do all right by myself. What a commitment!

When it was all over, and I was apologizing for my impatience and for the way I treated him at times, I jokingly said, "I know what you're thinking: 'If Lisa ever needs to move in the future, she'd better not ask me to help! I would never want to go through this again!' Right?"

David answered without thinking. "I would never say that. If you ever needed me again, I'd come right back and help you. This really wasn't so bad."

What a great brother! He rearranged everything in his life that month in order to help me, and he would turn around and do it again if I asked him.

What a lucky sister I am!

Scripture

In the Book of Ruth is a story about Naomi, a widow with two daughters-in-law, Orpah and Ruth. All three of them were widows, without any sons. This was a terrible predicament to be in because women in those days didn't have any rights. Without a husband or a son, a woman really was not safe or secure. Naomi told her two daughters-in-law to return to their families to find new husbands, because they were still young. She was old, however, and she would remain to find someone to live with.

It was a very tearful good-bye. Orpah left to return to her family, but Ruth did not. She said to Naomi: "Don't ask me to leave you! Let me go with you. Wherever you go, I will go; wherever you live, I will live. Your people will be my people, and your God will be my God" (Ruth 1:16, GNB).

To make a long story short, Ruth did find another husband. She became the great-grandmother of David, Israel's greatest king, and one of her descendants was Jesus.

Ruth, like my brother David, made a commitment to a family member that she cared about.

Reflections

Besides parents, do you have a family member that you are close to? a brother or sister, an aunt or uncle, a cousin, a grandmother or grandfather?

How did you become so close? How has this family member helped you with situations or difficult times that you couldn't handle alone?

Have you ever helped out or supported a family member during a difficult time? What were the circumstances?

Made in God's Own Image

My best friend in college was named David. I met him in acting class, and I immediately liked him. Except for our first year, we always lived in the same dorm; and except for one semester, we always had at least one class together.

We often studied together. I was a psychology major, and he had a double major—psychology and fine arts.

One time I called him on the phone to ask him about something from one of our classes. This was unusual; we didn't often call each other. It was just as quick to run up or down the steps and knock on the door. But this time I called. Good thing I did.

I said, "I'm coming down for help with this chapter, okay?"

David was in a panic. "Oh, no, no. You cannot come down right now. Oh, no. This would be a very bad time. I am too shy."

This was unlike David. "Why? What are you doing?"

"Oh, I would be too embarrassed to have you come in now."

"Well, now you have me curious . . ."

"Well, it wouldn't be proper, you know. I'm not exactly dressed. And the room is fixed up just so, you know."

"No, I don't know. What are you talking about?"

"Didn't I tell you? I'm working on *the sketch*."

David was always working on something. He was extremely talented. He did paintings, woodcuts, pen-and-ink drawings, and the like. Talent just poured out through his hands.

I couldn't recall which sketch he had told me about. But obviously I was supposed to know what he was working on and why I couldn't come visit him. So I asked him to remind me of exactly what the subject matter of *the sketch* was.

"Don't you remember? It's the nude."

Oh! The nude! I remembered! His assignment was to draw a nude, either of himself, of a famous Greek statue, or of one of those human doll figures that artists have that can be bent into different positions for drawing. David had one of those. Every time I went into his room, I would position it doing something different—dancing with a pencil, trying to climb out of the sock drawer, sitting on top of the deodorant can, and the like.

"So, what did you decide to do? Are you sitting in front of a mirror with no clothes on? Is that why I can't come over?"

Silence.

"Really? Is that it? Did I guess it?"

"Yes, yes. But this is no good. I am too thin. I don't make a good model. I am sitting here trying to think about what to do. I had two thoughts. I could draw myself, then put someone else's face on my head. Then no one would know it was a self-portrait. . . ."

I laughed.

"Or I could draw the famous *David,* by Michelangelo, and then draw my face on his head. And I could title it 'David, a self-portrait.' That might be a bit more impressive, don't you think?"

"I think your body is fine. I think that if you decide to sketch your head on someone else's body, or your body with someone else's head, it won't be because there's anything wrong with your body."

"Well, I don't know. But I'd better get back to *the sketch.*"

We decided to get together later to study. But I snuck down to his room and slid a paper under his door. It was a face with a big smile, and it was saying, "Wow! David! What a body! Made in the image and likeness of God!"

He wouldn't open the door, but I could hear him laughing.

Scripture

Faith
Fits

God created human persons in God's own image; in the image of God were they created; male and female God created them. God blessed them.

(Genesis 1:27–28, in *Scripture Readings,* page 349)

Reflections

Why are people so often dissatisfied with the way they look? Do you believe that God thinks you are beautiful the way you are? Why or why not? What do you like most about your body?

The Biggest of All Plants

Mother's Day was coming, and I asked my friend Frances what she was going to do for her mother. She told me that she was going to get her some kind of plant. I thought that sounded like a good idea. So we made plans to go to some plant stores the day before Mother's Day.

Frances had the family car that day, so she picked me up. We also picked up two other friends, Mike and Bob. They weren't looking for plants, but we often did things together just for fun.

The first store we walked into had a little cactus in a squatty pot. It was short and thick, but I could tell that it was very healthy. I knew my mom liked cactus plants, so I immediately chose it. "This is what I'll get."

Mike and Bob and Fran thought I was crazy!

"If I gave that ugly thing to my mother, she'd hit me over the head with it!" Mike said.

"How do you know it isn't dead?" Frances asked.

"It doesn't even look real. What if you find out it's plastic?" Bob asked.

They laughed at me, and I laughed, too. But I knew my mother would love it. So I stuck with my choice.

And I was right. She did love it.

That was twenty years ago.

I assure you, that little chunk of cactus was not dead. And it was not plastic. It still stands in our house, about nine feet tall now. Every so often it blooms with huge white flowers the size of your hand. We're lucky we have a room with a ceiling high enough to hold it. Every time I visit, I have to check it out to see how it's doing. Over the years, as it bloomed, my mom would take pictures to send to me so I could see how it looked. We wouldn't trade it for anything.

Scripture

Faith
Fits Jesus said to his disciples:

> With what can we compare the [Reign] of God, or
> what parable will we use for it? It is like a mustard
> seed, which, when sown upon the ground, is the
> smallest of all the seeds on earth; yet when it is sown
> it grows up and becomes the greatest of all shrubs,
> and puts forth large branches, so that the birds of
> the air can make nests in its shade.
>
> (Mark 4:30–33, NRSV)

Reflections

Sometimes it's the little things in life that are important.
It's the little things that we remember that can teach us
big lessons.

Did you ever plant a seed as a child? Do you remember how exciting it was when it started to grow? Why was
that so exciting? What did you learn from it?

What's a little thing from your life that you used to
think was insignificant but you now realize is important?

Light a Candle!

I have some close friends who live in Chicago. I don't get to see them often, but when I do, it's delightful.

Once when I was visiting them, I went to a party to meet their friends. They wanted me to meet someone in particular, a guy named Simon. But Simon was out of town.

Well, it seemed that everyone at the party knew Simon. They all asked me, "Have you met Simon?" I heard stories, I saw pictures, and I assured everyone that someday I would come back to Chicago, and I would most definitely meet this Simon. He sounded like a wonderful guy.

My days in Chicago flew by. The day I left, I heard some awful news. Simon had been mugged! He had been coming out of a cafe the previous night, and a man with a knife, who seemed to be just waiting in the parking lot, came running up to him and started stabbing and cutting up his arm. Then he ran away and left Simon to bleed in the parking lot. Simon made his way back into the cafe, and he was taken to the hospital for treatment.

"Why would someone do such a thing?" I wondered out loud.

"It's gay bashing," they told me. "That cafe is known to be a hangout for homosexuals. That mugger was just waiting to cut up anyone who came out the door."

I felt sick over this. The wonderful Simon I had heard so much about had had to go through such an ordeal.

My friends took me to the airport, and we said our good-byes. I asked them to let me know how Simon was coming along. They said they would.

Back in the plane, flying home, I couldn't stop thinking about Simon. I felt as if I knew him. Why should someone be attacked just because of a sexual orientation? From what I had heard about Simon, he would never hurt anyone.

I thought about my gay friends in Chicago and in Nebraska. I thought of how frightening it must be to live most of your life trying to hide who you are from most of the people you know, living a double life from fear of rejection—not to mention fear of getting sliced up with a knife.

Flying way up in the clouds, some place between Illinois and Nebraska, I thought of Simon again. I began to cry silently. Then I began to sob. Uncontrollably. It is a good thing those planes are so noisy, because that way no one heard me. I couldn't figure out how to stop crying. All the injustice of the entire world just seemed to well up in my eyes. It was all so unfair.

Eventually I figured out that I was crying from helplessness. The world of prejudice was so big and so unmanageable. What could I possibly do? Simon didn't even know me. I was a complete stranger.

Then, all of a sudden, it hit me. I was a complete stranger! The man who attacked Simon was a complete stranger! I could do something that no one else who knew Simon could do. I made plans in the sky. By the time I realized that I had stopped crying, I was already smiling.

When I got home, I called my friends in Chicago. I told them my plan. They gave me Simon's address. Here's what I did.

I bought a cuddly little teddy bear and wrapped its one arm up in a bandage. Then I wrote a note to go along with it. The note said something like this:

> I know you don't know me, but I heard what happened to you, and I feel terrible. I thought that if you knew about a complete stranger who cared about you, then maybe it might help to balance out the fear of knowing about a complete stranger who tried to hurt you. Maybe someday I'll get to meet you.

It wasn't long before I heard from my friends again. Simon had gotten the present and was really touched. I know it wasn't much, but it was something. And doing something is always better than doing nothing.

By the way, I finally did meet Simon—in New Jersey, of all places! I was visiting my mother, and she had gotten tickets to see a show that Simon was in. I wrote ahead to him and told him that I'd come backstage after the show so we could meet. He was as sweet as everyone said he was. He showed me the scars on his arm. I'm already looking forward to my next trip to Chicago, whenever that will be!

Scripture

You are the light of the world.

(Matthew 5:14, NAB)

It's better to light one candle than curse the darkness.

(Motto of the Christopher Society)

Reflections

Crying in that plane made me feel as if I were trapped in the darkness. But as soon as I thought of one small thing I could do for Simon, it felt as if one candle had been lit. It was a tiny candle, but even one candle is enough to make the darkness less frightening.

What's the biggest darkness in your life? What's one small thing you can do to light a candle and make it a little brighter?

Has anyone ever lit a candle for you in your darkness? Who was it? What was the occasion?

Imagine if everyone you know tried to light a candle every time they were faced with darkness. Wouldn't that make a big difference in the world? Why don't people just do it?

The Dance I Never Went To

Works LifeWhen I was a sophomore at Union Catholic High School, I wanted nothing more than to go to the school's winter dance. All my friends were talking about whom they were going with, where they would be eating dinner, and what dress they would wear, and I really wanted to be a part of this excitement.

So I asked a guy to the dance. But he turned me down. That was okay. I figured I would think of someone else I could ask. So I asked another guy to the dance. He turned me down, too. Well, that was a little harder to take, but I still wanted to go. So I asked another guy to the dance. He turned me down, too.

This was getting embarrassing. I wasn't having much luck with this. But I asked another guy to the dance. He turned me down, too. That didn't stop me either! I asked another guy! and another guy! and another guy! and another guy!

And I got turned down and turned down and turned down and turned down!

I am quite certain that I now hold the world's record for the most guys asked by one girl to a dance that she never attended—nine.

I cried my eyes out for days. I thought it was going to be the end of the world. But it wasn't.

I did eventually go to a dance, but not until my junior year. I went with a marvelous guy who was cute and funny and fun. His name was Mike. Listen to how we met. We were at a party, and he came over to talk to me because he thought I was someone else. As soon as he saw the girl that he thought I was, he sort of excused himself and walked away. Quite suddenly!

It's hard to believe that he and I became such good friends, isn't it? But we did! Now we think about those days and laugh.

In high school I didn't have very good luck with romance. But I'm happily married now, with two wonderful sons. Sometimes things happen, and we think we can never live through the embarrassment. But we do.

And eventually the same things that made us cry can make us laugh. Funny how life works.

Scripture

Faith
Fits
If you think being turned down by nine guys for one dance is bad, wait until you hear this Bible story about a teenager named Sarah.

Sarah was young and beautiful. What was her problem? She had been married seven times, and each time she got married, her husband died in bed just before they were about to have sex! But God sent an angel to help Tobias, the eighth husband, get rid of the demon that was killing off the husbands.

If you'd like to know the whole story, just read the Book of Tobit.

Reflections

Have you ever been turned down by someone you asked out? What was it like? How did you feel?

Has anyone ever asked you for a date or a dance, and you turned them down? What was that like? How did you feel saying no?

Do you believe that there is only one love meant for each of us? Or do you think that there might be lots of people that any of us could choose from and be happy with?

Happy Birthday to You

A long time ago, when my brothers and I were little kids, we were celebrating my dad's birthday. Of course we had a birthday cake and candles and singing and presents. After we sang and my dad blew out the candles, my mom went to get a cake knife and some plates. My dad got impatient waiting for her, and he used his finger to swipe a glob of icing from the top of the cake and then licked it off his finger. My brother Joey thought that was a good idea, so he started to do the same thing. But my dad grabbed his hand in midmotion, and said, "Joey, don't do that!"

Joey looked at him with big brown eyes. "Why not? You just did it!"

My dad paused. Joey was right. But he could see where this could get out of hand. So he responded with confidence, "That's because today is my birthday, not yours. Everyone can't be licking the icing off the cake. When it's your birthday, you can lick the icing."

Joey and the rest of us accepted that "Daddy logic." So we waited for our piece of cake, and then we used forks, not fingers.

That took place in the month of March.

Now we'll fast-forward to the month of June, on the day of Joey's birthday. The scene is similar. We had the birthday candles and the singing and the presents. After we sang, Joey blew out the candles, and we were waiting for Mom to come with the plates and the cake knife.

Joey looked up at Dad, smiled, and stuck his fingers into the cake, taking not only a swipe of icing but a handful of the cake as well.

Dad yelled, "Joey, don't do that!"

Joey looked at him again with the big brown eyes. "Why not? You said I could do it when it was my birthday."

The rest of us were looking up at him with our big brown eyes as well. "You did, Dad. We all heard you. You said it on your birthday."

Even Mom agreed with us.

"Okay, then, if I said you could, then you can. Whenever it's your birthday, you get first swipe at the icing!"

And that's how one of our family traditions got started.

I have two sons of my own, and at our house, when we're celebrating a birthday, we get reminded, "Don't forget to stick your finger in the icing!"

We've even done it at birthday parties outside of our family. We have to do some explaining, but that's okay. It keeps alive an important family tradition!

Scripture

Faith Fits

So then, brothers and sisters, stand firm and hold fast to the traditions that you were taught by us, either by word of mouth or by our letter.

(2 Thessalonians 2:15, NRSV)

Reflections

Obviously our family's birthday cake tradition is not understood by everyone. If we were visiting some friends who had made a cake to celebrate one of our birthdays, and we just swiped off the icing before the cake was served, it would be rude not to explain the tradition.

That's what happens sometimes in our faith. A lot of our rituals had great meaning many years ago when they were begun. But now, if we don't talk about why we do what we do, the meaning is lost.

What are some of the traditions of the church that you don't understand?

Do you think you would appreciate them more if you knew the stories behind them?

Who could you ask for an explanation?

Peace on Earth

The following are notes from two Christmas cards sent to me by my high school friend Bob:

> Christmas is sipping eggnog while warming your feet and your heart by a crackling fire. The lights are out, the family is in bed, and snow silently falls outside the window. Sweetly sung carols can be heard in the distance—or perhaps it is childhood echoing in your mind. You smile, and breathe in the fragrances of pine and cinnamon, burning wood, and the last drops of eggnog in the bottom of your glass.
> Bob (December 1975)

> Christmas and your friendship are the same kind of thing. I don't think I could live without them, even if I don't show it all the time. It's easy to take great things for granted.
> Love always,
> Bob (December 1978)

Scripture

The angel said to [the shepherds], "Don't be afraid! I am here with good news for you, which will bring great joy to all the people. This very day in David's town your Savior was born—Christ the Lord! And this is what will prove it to you: you will find a baby wrapped in cloths and lying in a manger."

Suddenly a great army of heaven's angels appeared with the angel, singing praises to God:
"Glory to God in the highest heaven,
    and peace on earth."

(Luke 2:10–14, GNB)

Reflections

For shepherds, angels, and friends like Bob, Christmas-time can bring out the deepest of feelings.

How do you usually feel around Christmastime? Are you excited and filled with joy? Or are you depressed with the stress, the rushing around, and the dilemma of trying to figure out which presents to buy for which people? What would be the "perfect" Christmas for you?

Outward Appearances

My first year in college, I took an acting class. I had enjoyed acting in high school, and I wanted to keep doing it.

We often had acting assignments. We would have to practice scenes with other students in the class, and then perform them for a grade.

Usually we were given a choice of scenes with two or three characters and different combinations of male and female parts. We could also choose to do a monolog—a scene with just one person acting. The professor didn't really care what combination we chose as long as everyone had at least one part to play for their grade.

I wanted to get to know this good-looking guy in the class, so I asked him if he'd do a scene with me. His name was Jeff. He said okay, so we set up a few times to rehearse. Another guy in the class asked me to do the same scene with him, but I really didn't want to. Keith was overweight and not very tall, and I was glad I had already asked Jeff.

Well, Jeff got into the habit of not showing up for class, and of not showing up to rehearse his part with me. I was getting a little nervous about my grade for the course. I called him several times, and he promised he would come through.

But he didn't. He finally showed up the night before our scene was due, but he told me he was going to do a different scene with some other girl instead. He hadn't even learned my scene or memorized the lines. He had known this for a while, but he didn't tell me—not even when I called him.

I was furious. Who was I going to find the day before our scene was due? I would have to memorize one of the monologs. I was afraid it was going to take me all night.

There I was at Fenwick Theater, it was close to midnight, and I was trying to learn all these new lines and to block out my scene. I was so angry, I could hardly think.

In the quiet I could hear footsteps coming down the hallway. Who would be here at this hour? At first I was just curious. But then I became frightened because I could hear the steps getting closer and closer. They stopped. The door opened. It was Keith. He had brought a thermos of coffee and a box of donuts! "I heard you got dumped, so I thought you might need some help," he explained.

I was so relieved to see him. I told him I was trying to memorize the monolog. He asked me, "Why don't you do the scene you were going to do with Jeff? I'd be happy to do it with you. I already know the lines."

I asked him, "Aren't you doing it with someone else?"

"Of course, that's why I know the lines. But I don't mind performing it twice. It would be awful for you to have to memorize a whole monolog tonight."

I thanked him, took a donut, drank some coffee, thanked him again, and we began to work out the scene together. We finished by about 3:00 a.m. I was glad to drop into bed that night.

Before falling asleep, I thought about Keith and Jeff. Why had I paid so much attention to the outward appearance and missed what was in the heart?

Scripture

When God told Samuel to go to Jesse's house to choose the next king, Samuel was ready to meet the whole family. Jesse's oldest son stepped forward, and he was handsome. Samuel was sure this would be God's choice for the next king. But God cautioned Samuel:

> Do not look on his appearance or on the height of his stature, because I have rejected him; for I see not as flesh sees; you look on the outward appearance, but I look on the heart.
>
> (1 Samuel 16:7, in *Scripture Readings*, page 124)

Samuel looked at each one of Jesse's sons, but God did not want any of them. He asked Jesse, "Do you have another son?" Jesse called David in from the fields. He was very young. But God told Samuel that David was the one.

Reflections

Have you ever wanted to get to know someone because they were good looking, only to be disappointed? What happened?

Did you ever dismiss someone because of their unattractive looks, only to discover later that they were really quite wonderful? What happened?

It Can't Be Done

My dad was some guy. He could pretty much figure out how to do anything he wanted to do. In fact, it was a family joke not to utter "It can't be done" around my dad, or he would spend the next month or so proving you wrong.

I guess I internalized that a bit as I grew up. Not that I had to prove to anyone that I could do everything. But when I was considering something, and I thought that I could do it, the challenge of "It can't be done" was enough to motivate me to try.

After I graduated from high school, I went looking for a summer job. I wanted to go into teaching, so I thought that being a summer camp counselor would be the perfect way to gain some experience with children. Even though I had never worked at a camp before, I got lucky and found a job because another counselor had dropped out at the last minute. It was a fun job.

At the end of the summer, I was told that their only opening the following year would be for a trained pool counselor. For that job I would need to be a Red Cross lifeguard and swimming instructor. I said, "Okay. I'll take that job." The camp director questioned, "You're a lifeguard and swimming instructor?" I answered confidently, "I will be by next summer."

The camp director laughed at me. That was bad enough. But then he said those four words, "It can't be done!"

I just smiled. He didn't know my dad. He didn't know me, either.

I went home and told my dad what had happened. He said, "Let's get one of their books and see what we can learn." So, with a Red Cross book on swimming skills in his hand, my dad coached me for several weeks before my college classes began. And I swam laps and laps and laps.

Okay, I wasn't great. My form wasn't perfect. But I was good enough to pass the test so I could take the life-saving course at the YMCA in the city where I attended college. I also enrolled in their stroke and endurance clinic, which was an intense class that taught all the basic strokes and coached you to swim with better form.

My college friends watched me get up early to swim laps and then go to the pool in the evening for class. They asked me, "Isn't there another job at another camp that might be easier for you to get?" They didn't understand. I was challenged. I was told that "it couldn't be done." My family honor was at stake here. Besides, I had discovered that I really enjoyed swimming!

So I passed the lifesaving class and became a Red Cross lifeguard. Then I tried out for the Water Safety Instructor course. I passed the test to get into the class, and then I passed the class. I had done it!

Not only did I have quite a career as a swimming counselor at several fine summer camps throughout my college years, but I even joined the Holy Cross college swim team in my junior year. When I was a senior, I was the only senior on the team, so at graduation I was the Outstanding Senior of the swim team! I was even given a watch that says "Holy Cross Crusaders" on it. I still have that watch. It means a lot to me.

All because some camp director who didn't know any better said, "It can't be done."

Scripture

[Jesus told his disciples,] "I say to you, if you have faith the size of a mustard seed, you will say to this mountain, 'Move from here to there,' and it will move. Nothing will be impossible for you."

(Matthew 17:20, NAB)

Reflections

What has been your biggest challenge? What was something you accomplished that you never thought was possible? What was it like? How did you pull it off?

What do you think is one of the world's greatest problems? What would everyone have to do to solve this problem? Do you think it would be possible if everyone did their part? Or do you think that "it can't be done"?

Parents' Love

Life
Works

When I was a senior in high school, I went on a four-day retreat called Christian Encounter. During this retreat we received letters of support from other people we knew at school who had gone on the same retreat. We also received a letter from our parents. I still have all those letters. Here is an excerpt from the letter from my parents:

> To my dearest grown-up baby daughter Lisa,
> Your Dad and I were children at a time when love was expressed through sacrifice and action rather than with words. So we rarely express in words what you surely know is in our hearts. Every action, every decision we make, no matter how disappointing to you at the time, is motivated by our love and our desire to protect you.
>
> A human baby is born helpless, completely dependent upon a mother and father's love for its life and protection. From that moment on, the child strives for independence, and many conflicts develop. But the power of a strong love with God's help eventually leads to understanding and peace.
>
> Dad and I are very happy that you are enjoying life to its fullest. Our many fears, however, cause us to continue to guide and restrict your pathways. Please forgive us, for our love forces us to protect that which we hold most precious.
> Our love always,
> Mom and Dad

I'll tell you something. I was not an easy teenager to deal with. My parents and I had a lot of arguments as I tried to "find myself." I know I caused them a lot of pain and frustration.

Now that I am an adult, I can look at the way my life turned out, and I can see my mother and father's influence in so much of what I say and do. I have been blessed abundantly.

My mom still calls me every Saturday morning. We usually talk for an hour or so. If I'm not home when she calls, she calls back! We hate to miss that weekly visit.

There is nothing like a parent's love—except maybe God's love.

Scripture

Faith Fits God has honored parents with children, giving them
authority over their sons and daughters.
Children who honor their parents atone for sins,
those who revere them are like one who lays up
treasure.
Children who honor their parents will be gladdened
by their own children,
and when they pray, they will be heard.
Those who glorify their father and mother will have
long life,
and those who obey God will bring new life to
their parents.
(Sirach 3:2–6, in *Scripture Readings,* page 53)

Reflections

Many different kinds of families exist: traditional families, stepfamilies, blended families, foster families, adoptive families, and even combinations of these.

In your unique family, how is your relationship with your parents? What has your mother or father done for you that shows how much you are loved? Do you ever take this love for granted? What happens? What are the things that you do to show your love for your family?

Working on Your Day Off

My brother Joe and I visited some friends one Sunday afternoon. Bill and Kara had just bought their first house, and we were driving over to check it out. Tim, a friend of ours, came with us.

We had all worked hard that week, and we were looking forward to a relaxing day. It had been a while since we had gotten together, and this promised to be a fun time.

When we arrived it seemed that Bill and Kara were a bit behind on their work. They were putting up a fence and having a terrible time with it. It seemed to be a job that they couldn't accomplish alone.

Immediately, my brother Joe offered to help. He rolled up his sleeves and got right into it. He had had a bit of experience with this sort of thing before, and he was able to figure out what needed to be done. He enjoyed feeling useful.

Tim pitched in also, but it was clear that he wasn't as enthusiastic about getting involved. He thought he was going to be able to relax and kick back. This was his weekend time, his free time, his time to unwind. He was obviously annoyed at having to work.

I just hung around and watched and did what I was asked to do: "Hold this." "Get that." Not knowing much about fences, I was happy to take care of any little thing I could manage. It was really kind of fun. I learned a lot about fences and gardening and soil, and we enjoyed one another's company while we worked together.

Except for Tim. He was pretty unhappy all day.

When it was over and we were driving home, I just kept thinking about how the day had turned out. I was really impressed with Joe's willingness to do such hard work on his day off. I am sure he thought nothing of it. And that makes it even more admirable. I remember thinking that I wanted to be more like him. I wanted to be ready to help whenever I was needed, and I wanted to be glad to do it.

Scripture

Faith
Fits
Jesus knew the importance of the Sabbath. The Sabbath is a day for rest. It is a day when all labor and work is put aside so that each person is free to pray, to think about God, and to be thankful for all her or his blessings.

But Jesus also understood people's real needs. He pointed out that people's real needs have to be attended to, even if they occur on one's day off, even if that day is the Sabbath. (See Luke 13:10–17 and Luke 14:1–6.)

Reflections

Do you hate to do work around the house on a day off from school? Do you feel like those days are your free days, and you shouldn't have to do any chores? Why or why not?

Do you like to get all your chores done right away so you have unpressured free time to enjoy? Or do you put off all your chores and do other things you enjoy first?

Do your parents have to remind you to do your chores, or are you responsible enough to take care of them on your own?

Death Row

I have two pen pals who are on death row. One of them is Jack, who has a young daughter. He doesn't get to see her very often, and he mentions how he misses her in almost every letter. His letters are chatty, and he likes to talk. He calls us collect once a month. He likes to talk to my sons, Michael and Ralph, about sports and school. They even write to him occasionally. And he always writes back and answers all their questions.

The other pen pal, Sam, is younger. He is in a different prison, and is not allowed to make phone calls. His letters are reflective, almost poetic at times. One time he mentioned waking up early and hearing the birds outside a window—nature sounds that reminded him of freedom and the fullness of life. He contrasted those sounds with what he heard next—the slamming of the steel doors of the prison, reminding him that his life was neither free nor full. Another time he told me that he was able to see the space shuttle launch from his window. It was breathtaking for him to have been able to witness that. Even as a caged prisoner, he felt privileged to share in that slice of history and greatness.

You can forget any stereotypes about "people in prison." They are as different and multifaceted as people on the outside.

Sam and Jack have educated me a great deal. They send me articles that explain the legal system, and they describe the death-row situation from the lawyer's point of view as well as from the prisoner's point of view.

Eventually I discovered that Sam's family didn't live that far from me, and I became friends with his mother. We got together a couple of times to talk, share stories, and cry a little. She gave me a picture of Sam as a high school senior. He's an attractive guy with hope and joy in his eyes. It's hard to believe how such a person could end up on death row. But it happens.

According to Fr. Bill O'Malley, "God loves us as helplessly as a mother loves her child on death row" (*The People's Catechism*, page 26). I understand what that means, because I have seen that helpless love with my own eyes.

I have been inspired by Sam and Jack, and by their families' struggle, patience, positive attitude, even humor, and especially by their faith.

Eventually I was able to meet both of them. I visited the prisons where they spend their days, one in Florida and the other in Illinois. I continue to write to them, to pray for them and their families, and also to pray for all victims and victims' families.

Life is complicated. Sometimes people grow up in difficult circumstances, learn tough lessons, and do horrible things. When a person is murdered, the victim's family is never the same again. And neither is the family of the murderer.

Not everyone on death row is a murderer. Some are wrongly accused, some have poor legal counsel, and many are trapped in the system's slow-moving procedures and policies. There's no easy answer, and no shortcut to the truth.

Scripture

Faith
Fits I was in prison, and you visited me.

(Matthew 25:36, NRSV)

Remember those who are in prison, as though you were in prison with them.

(Hebrews 13:3, NRSV)

Jesus knew about prison and death row—he was executed between two other criminals: a humble one who repented and a proud one who did not. Jesus forgave the humble one, and promised that they would meet in heaven that very day.

Reflections

Have you ever been inside a jail or prison? What do you think it would be like to get into serious trouble with the law? What do you think the worst part about being in jail might be?

Would you ever want to become a pen pal with a person on death row? Why or why not?

One Handy Guy

Ever since we were little, our parents always had us make cards and presents to give to people instead of buying them.

Why was it so important for children to learn how to make things? I think it was because of the time and thought it takes. If we were given money as little kids, we probably would just buy the first thing we saw that was "nice." We might buy the first card we saw, not even understanding what it said inside.

When we make something for someone, we take time to create, and also to think of the person as we are creating. It's a more active process of love.

Anyway, we learned the lesson well. As adults we still try to make a lot of our gifts. We buy things, too, but a lot of creativity goes into what we give one another.

Here's one of my favorite examples: It was Father's Day. My brother Steven handed my dad a two-part present. Dad opened up the first part. It was a cassette tape.

But it was no ordinary tape. It was a recording of a "tribute" to my handy dad. Steven whipped out a tape player, and we all listened to it right away. It used every "hand" pun thinkable. Things such as: "Dad's always there to give us a helping hand . . ." and "Dad is so handy . . ." and "I've really got to hand it to you, Dad . . ." The tribute ended something like this: "So now, let's all put our hands together and give a big hand to our wonderful handy dad!" and then we heard an audience applauding on the tape!

Then Steven gave Dad the second part of the present —a hand! A large hand made of metal or plastic or something. I just thought that it was one of the most clever presents I had ever seen.

The fun continued, too. That hand showed up all over the house in strange places, secretly placed to surprise whoever came upon it. It found its way into the bathroom, holding a towel; into the refrigerator, holding a can of fruit; into the living room, "climbing" up from behind the couch; and into other surprising locations.

What made that gift so loving (as well as entertaining)? Obviously Steven cared about Dad. He knew him, he thought about him, and he showed his love with praise and admiration. I think that's what gift giving is really all about.

Scripture

Israel and Judah, what am I going to do with you? Your love for me disappears as quickly as morning mist; it is like dew, that vanishes early in the day. That is why I have sent my prophets to you with my message of judgment and destruction. What I want from you is plain and clear: I want your constant love, not your animal sacrifices. I would rather have my people know me than have them burn offerings to me.

(Hosea 6:4–6, GNB)

Reflections

What kind of presents do you like to receive? What was the best or most unique present you ever received? What made it so special?

What kind of presents do you like to give? What was the best or most unique present you ever gave to anyone?

What's a more precious thing to give to someone— a lot of time or a lot of money? Why?

Graduation Celebrations

During my junior year in high school, I was active in the drama club. So were my three best friends: Mike, Bob, and Fran. We had been in several shows together, and had become close friends with the seniors who also were in drama. When it came time for them to graduate, we wanted to do something special for them.

It was Bob's idea to plan a Mass for them. Not at a church or at our school but at someone's home, with a big party to follow it.

I was known as the group's poet, so Bob asked me to write a poem for the event. Mike was known as the group's artist, so Bob asked him to create a banner for the event. Bob and Fran were in charge of most of the other details.

Our parents were a little surprised that our gift to one another would be something as "holy" as a Mass. And our senior friends were very touched.

We picked the readings, picked the songs, and even wrote a program.

The cover of the program had the rainbow artwork that Mike had designed for the banner. Across Mike's rainbow backdrop were the words to the poem I wrote, a sonnet:

> The time has come to leave your dreams of
>   childhood,
> To venture forth where new horizons lie;
> To know you must walk boldly toward the future
> And part with friends, yet bid them not good-bye.
> The times ahead are filled with new beginnings
> And each of you will go a separate way,
> Giving of yourselves where e'er you travel,
> Yet keeping all the blessings of today.
> Our gift to you is one that's very simple:
> A wish for luck in challenges to come,
> A word of praise for all that you will do,
> And thanks for all that you've already done.
> And as you depart, your lives to elsewhere live,
> We give you all the love that's ours to give.

Even though I wrote this poem more than twenty years ago, I still give it as a gift to graduating seniors every year.

Scripture

Faith
Fits
Be joyful always, pray at all times, be thankful in all circumstances.

(1 Thessalonians 5:16–18, GNB)

Reflections

How would you react if one of your friends came up with the idea of giving a Mass-party for your graduating senior friends?

How would you react if your friends came up with the idea of giving you a Mass-party for your graduation present?

You Are God's Temple

I was in the locker room at the pool where I used to be a lifeguard. Three teenage girls I knew were also there. They were getting dressed after a swim and looking at themselves in the mirror. None of them was overweight by any stretch of the imagination. But here is a sample of their comments:

"I'm so fat! Look at this blubber! I hate my body."

"Oh, yeah? Look at this stomach! It sticks out. I am gross."

"Look at these thighs! and this butt! I wish I could just remove one big chunk of my body—you know, just lop off some flesh and throw it away!"

At that point a new girl came into the locker room, wearing long sweatpants over her bathing suit. I had never seen her before. Neither had the three girls getting dressed.

She smiled and said, "Hi."

We all smiled back and said, "Hi."

She leaned against the wall, pulled down her sweatpants just a bit, did some twisting or adjusting or something, and then, "plop!" off came her sweatpants, along with her entire left leg.

She left the artificial leg in the corner, smiled at us, and confidently hopped out and dove gracefully into the pool.

The three girls were completely silent.

That was the last time I ever heard any one of them utter anything about not liking their body and wishing a chunk of flesh could be lopped off.

Scripture

Faith
Fits

Do you not know that you are God's temple and that God's Spirit dwells in you? . . . For God's temple is holy, and you are that temple.

(1 Corinthians 3:16–17, NRSV)

Reflections

Young women feel a lot of pressure these days to be overly thin. It isn't healthy. Anorexia and bulimia are the result of the thin ideal. On the other hand, eating junk food and not getting any exercise is not healthy, either.

Our body is the temple of the Holy Spirit. Taking care of it is a way of praising and thanking God.

Do you take care of your body? Are you abusing it with tobacco or alcohol or other illegal drugs?

Do you eat too much or too little?

Do you need to exercise more or less?

What is one simple habit you need to change in order to take better care of your body, your temple of the Holy Spirit?

Rejected as Worthless

My husband has a decorative bowl and pitcher that has a lot of sentimental value for him. One time I asked him if I could borrow it for a prayer service with teenage leaders of our parish peer-ministry team. Washing one another's hands was to be part of the prayer. I thought that using a nice basin and pitcher would make the simple ritual look elegant and significant. He reluctantly said yes, with a warning for us to be very careful.

When the prayer was over, I was relieved that no one had dropped the pitcher as we poured the water over each person's hands. However, as I was cleaning up, I dropped the bowl. Even though it hit a carpeted floor, it still broke into many pieces. I just burst into tears. I couldn't believe I had done such a thing! I knew my husband hadn't really wanted me to use it. I knew it meant a lot to him. Why did I even ask him to let me use it?

I sat on the floor of my office and cried and cried. I didn't know what to do. I felt so sick inside. Eventually I began to collect the pieces and see if I could piece together the bigger ones. There were at least a dozen pieces, with lots of tiny shards too tiny to fit in. It used to look so lovely. It was a pale blue-green color with little delicate flowers painted all over it in different colors.

I finally called Ralph and told him what had happened. I was crying when he answered the phone, so I think he was relieved that the only tragedy I had to report was a broken bowl. But I know how upset he was with my clumsiness, even though he tried not to show it.

Well, I got some glue, and I decided to at least try to put together the pieces that were big enough to attach. It was not easy. There were so many pieces, and it was difficult to find the right piece to match each space.

When I finally finished, it was very ugly. The cracks were obvious, and tiny fragments were missing everywhere. It seemed truly worthless.

I brought it home and put it back on our shelf where it used to sit. Ralph didn't say much. Probably something like, "Oh, you tried to glue the bowl back together." He never mentioned it after that, but whenever I looked at it, it was a reminder of my carelessness, and I felt clumsy and careless.

A month or so later, while looking through a catalog, I happened to find a similar bowl and pitcher. The shape was identical, but the colors were different. I ordered it. I was hoping that Ralph might forgive me if I got him a new set. If he accepted my offering, at least I wouldn't have that reminder of ugliness, clumsiness, and carelessness staring at me daily in my own living room.

The new pitcher and bowl arrived. I wrapped it up carefully in a big box with lots of tissue paper—I wasn't taking any chances—and a gigantic bow. It was waiting for Ralph on the dining-room table when he came home. He said, "What's this?" and I answered, "Just open it."

So he did. And he took the two items out of the box and looked at me, perplexed. "Why did you buy this? What's this for?"

I sheepishly answered, "It's so you don't have such an ugly thing in the living room reminding you every day of how clumsy and careless your wife is."

He seemed surprised. He looked directly into my eyes. "Is that what you think I see whenever I look at the cracked one?"

"Of course! What else could you think?" I asked him.

"I'll tell you," he began. "Whenever I look at that bowl, and I see all those cracks all over it, going every which way, here's what I think. I think about how sad you were about breaking it, and about how much time and patience and care it took for you to put together all those pieces for me. Whenever I see that cracked bowl, I think about how lucky I am that you love me."

Well, suddenly that cracked and worthless bowl was the most beautiful item in the house! It wasn't a symbol of my failure at all! It was a symbol of love—a reminder of the biggest blessing in my life.

That bowl rejected as worthless has become the most valuable bowl we own! It still sits proudly in a place of honor in our living room.

I keep the new bowl and pitcher in my office now. If I ever want to use something nice for a prayer ritual that involves pouring water from a pitcher into a bowl, that's the set I'll use. The other one is too precious to risk.

Scripture

The stone which the builders rejected as worthless
  turned out to be the most important of all.
This was done by the Lord;
  what a wonderful sight it is!

(Psalm 118:22–23, GNB)

The stone mentioned in this psalm is a foreshadowing of Jesus. He is the Lord, the one rejected by the Roman rulers and the religious leaders of his time. They thought Jesus was worthless and insignificant. God clearly thought otherwise.

Reflections

What seemingly unimportant, worthless thing or situation ended up being quite significant in your life?

What suffering or struggle or brokenness in your life has helped you to grow and become a stronger, more mature, and more caring person?

Do you know anyone who you once thought to be worthless and insignificant, who turned out to be marvelous and quite significant after all?

One Mind, One Heart

During my senior year in high school, I had a lead in the fall play. I was Mrs. Hardcastle in *She Stoops to Conquer*. It was such a thrill. Almost every member of the cast was already a friend of mine. I took this seriously, and I started to memorize my lines right away. I wanted to do the best possible job.

I remember one dress rehearsal vividly. I was having trouble with one line and was a little frustrated. I also had to wear a ridiculous hat in the scene, a hat I had never practiced with before, and I had to concentrate to keep it from falling off my head.

Let me set the stage for you. In this scene I am having a stern conversation with Tim, while on the other side of the stage, Mary Beth is having a nonverbal exchange with Bob. Bob is playing my son, and Tim is playing Mary Beth's boyfriend. I'm trying to be stern, I'm trying to keep this ridiculous hat on, and I'm trying not to mess up the line that Tim has gone over and over with me right before the scene.

All of a sudden the audience starts laughing—really hard. Tim and I keep playing the scene and saying our lines, but by the way we look at each other, we know that neither of us can figure out what is so funny. At first, I thought they must be laughing at the hat. So I tried to play that up by dramatically adjusting the hat and exaggerating my annoyance with it. But I could tell that the hat wasn't what they were laughing at. So we finished the scene and went backstage.

We caught up with Bob and Mary Beth, and we asked them, "What was so funny?" Well it was the two of them! In the scene they were mad at each other, and they usually played it by just standing there with their arms crossed and looking angry and annoyed. But this time they got more creative. They started sticking their tongues out at each other, chasing each other around a couch, and throwing pillows at each other. It sounded hilarious. No wonder the audience was laughing so hard.

After the rehearsal, our director praised Bob and Mary Beth for making the scene come alive. Tim and I decided how we could say the important lines at the beginning and the end of the scene in a loud voice so the audience wouldn't miss them. The rest of the conversation was less important. That way the audience could enjoy Bob and Mary Beth's antics more. And Bob and Mary Beth would stop doing their thing right before our last lines so the audience could shift back their attention to us. We practiced it again to get the timing right.

Meanwhile, another actor who had observed the whole affair spoke up. He said that what we just did was terrible. Not only did we allow Bob and Mary Beth to upstage us and steal our scene but we cooperated with them and helped them do a better job of it the next time. He said we should have argued with the director that we had an important scene and that we didn't want to share it with some slapstick humor. Obviously we weren't "real actors," or we would have been more concerned with staying in the spotlight.

I looked at Tim, and asked him: "Do you think he's right? Did we do the wrong thing? I just figured that if the scene is funnier that way, then let's do it that way. Doesn't that make the play better?"

Tim agreed. "We're in this together. Why would we want to stop someone else from being funny? It's a comedy. It's supposed to be funny. I think real actors are the ones who can be of one mind and one heart with the whole cast. Then you have real acting."

Bob and Mary Beth came by. "We didn't mean to steal your scene," they said. I told them: "We're glad you did. You made it better."

Scripture

Faith Fits

The Acts of the Apostles is a book about the early church. It describes the followers of Jesus in this way: "The community of believers was of one mind and one heart. None of them claimed anything as their own; rather, everything was held in common" (Acts of the Apostles 4:32, INT).

Reflections

Have you ever felt upstaged? Do you have a brother or a sister who seems to get more attention than you do? Do other players on the basketball team get all the shots because you see who's open and pass the ball? They may get the points and the recognition, but you are the one who made it possible.

Is it wrong to feel jealousy? Or is it just wrong to act on it?

Have you ever been on a team or in the cast of a show or on a work crew with a group of people that you really enjoyed? Have you ever felt as if you completely belonged and your opinions and feelings and needs were as important as everyone else's? What was it like to be part of a group like that?

Get Involved

Works Life

My cousin Danny is the greatest storyteller. He can take a completely uneventful day and make it sound like an adventure. The reason he can do this so easily might be related to the fact that his whole life is an adventure.

I don't know anyone who lives a life like Danny's. Every time I talk to him, he tells me one more incredible story. Imagine looking through your camera's telephoto lens to try to capture a good picture, and then witnessing a major drug-smuggling operation. Imagine rescuing a stranger trapped in her car that had rolled over in the middle of the road. Imagine going for a leisurely ride in a boat on a lake and finding a dog in the middle of the lake—doggy-paddling of course—and trying to pull her up into your boat so you can identify the owner and return the missing pet. Imagine driving along and noticing a naked man running alongside the road, with blood all over his hands.

All these things are real events from Danny's life! How do all these things happen to him? *He gets involved.* He sees someone or something unusual, and he's curious, and he wants to help. Danny will literally stop whatever he is doing in order to give help to someone who needs it.

One time I was in a hurry, buying something at a drugstore, when I noticed a woman trying to talk with a clerk. The woman only spoke Spanish, and she was very frustrated. No one in the store seemed to know a single word of Spanish. My first thought was to just walk out and get going with all the things I had to do. But then I remembered my cousin Danny, who always stops to help people. So I went over and began to talk to the woman in Spanish. She started talking a mile a minute, and I couldn't understand a word she said. I had to slow her down and explain that I only knew a little Spanish, but I wanted to help. So back and forth we talked, and I realized that she needed to get some pink liquid medicine for her four-year-old granddaughter, who had a sore throat and no fever. We found what she needed, and she went on her way. It didn't take that long, and it made a big difference to this woman who felt all alone in a world where no one spoke her language.

I knew Danny would be proud of me.

Scripture

Faith
Fits

Do not neglect to show hospitality to strangers, for by doing that some have entertained angels without knowing it.

(Hebrews 13:2, NRSV)

Jesus tells a story in Luke's Gospel about a man who was robbed and beaten and left on the side of the road. Three different men walked by, but only the third one, a Samaritan, whom Jews were taught to despise and avoid, stopped to helped him.

Jesus asks us to be like that Samaritan and to do the same thing in our life. (Luke 10:25–37)

Reflections

Were you taught to not talk to strangers? If so, your parents were helping you to realize that not everyone in the world is your friend. Especially when you are alone, situations can occur in which it would be unsafe for you to get involved.

But other places and times are very safe. A "stranger" might be someone new at school, someone you are sitting next to in church, or someone who is buying groceries and trying to keep track of three young children at the same time. Reaching out to these people and offering a smile, a friendly greeting, and a helping hand would hardly be dangerous.

How do you react to "safe" strangers? Do you ignore the new person at school, or the person sitting next to you in church, or the person ahead of you in the grocery store line? Or do you greet them and make sure you are ready to assist them? Why?

Have you ever been in a difficult situation in which a stranger came along to help you? What happened?

Status and Labels

Life
Works

I am not a person who spends money on clothes with designer labels so that others will be impressed with how "cool" I am. But I know this is common in our materialistic culture.

With this in mind, I tried an experiment that I'd like to tell you about. When shopping in a thrift store, I found two pairs of shorts that were identical in every way—off-white in color, knitted fabric, with an elastic waist. Nothing was unusual about them, except that they both had labels on the front of them that said GUESS, and they were on sale for five dollars each.

So I bought both of them, and before wearing them, I removed one of the labels with a seam ripper. I wore the unlabeled shorts to a weekend youth event. I even asked several people, "So what do you think of my new shorts?" Most of the replies were lukewarm and uninterested: "Sure, yeah, they look okay, I guess." Or, "What's the big deal? They're just shorts."

The next day I wore the shorts that were exactly the same except for the designer label. I can't count how many teenagers commented: "Wow! Cool shorts!" and "I love those shorts. Where'd you get them?" and "Nice threads! You're looking good!"

Needless to say, everyone was shocked when they realized that the shorts they thought were so "boring" one day were the same ones they praised so highly the next day. What was the difference? A label! In other words, clothes are liked not because we actually like them but only because they have a label. It's like having a sign that says, "Notice: This will be seen as 'cool,' so like it."

My clothing experiment has worked several times, even in my own home with my teenage sons! And it works backward as well as forward. If I wear the shorts with the label on the first day, no one notices the identical shorts the following day, even if I point them out. Everyone is shocked to learn that they are the same design. I have to show them both pairs to prove it.

How have we gotten to this point as a society? Why do people get so excited about items of clothing with designer labels?

"What's the big deal? They're just shorts." It's a good question. Why isn't that our response all the time?

Scripture

Jesus tells us in the Gospel of Matthew:

> Why do you worry about clothing? Consider the lilies of the field, how they grow; they neither toil nor spin, yet I tell you, even Solomon in all his glory was not clothed like one of these.
>
> (6:28–29, NRSV)

Reflections

If people wear designer clothes to impress others, does it work? Are you really impressed? Are those people really the most impressive people you know? If not, why not? If so, what's so impressive besides the clothing?

If someone you dislike suddenly wears designer clothes, will you suddenly begin to like them? If someone you already like starts to wear "plain" clothes, will you stop liking them?

Do you think a "commonsense campaign" could be started to end the preoccupation with designer labels and expensive clothes? Why or why not? Besides saving money, what other benefits would it bring?

You Are Growing

A young woman in my youth group was having a few struggles as she tried to figure out whom she wanted to be, what she wanted to do with her life, and how to make some kind of difference in the world. Some days everything was wonderful, and other days everything was terrible.

During this same time, my brother Steve was having similar struggles. I realized as I listened to both of them talk to me on the same day that we never grow out of that. We never stop trying to figure out whom we want to be, what we want to do, and how to make a difference. Our life is always filled with great days and awful days. Growing older doesn't make it any easier, it just makes us more aware of the struggles and better able to articulate what they are. But we're still struggling! That part never goes away.

So I wrote this poem for my brother Steve and my young friend Amy. I wrote on Amy's note, "To Amy," and she asked me if, whenever I wrote this poem again, I would call it "To Amy." I told her I would.

To Amy
Your eyes are wide with dreams of what you want
        your world to be.
Your mind is full of images that no one else can see.
Some things you dearly try to change; some things
        you keep the same;
Trying to decide if life's a challenge or a game.

Sometimes you feel so lonely in a room that's filled
        with friends.
Sometimes you want to be alone where no one can
        pretend.
You long for a relationship to give your life some
        wealth.
I can see you're struggling; I struggle, too, myself.

We each have different talents, and we bloom in
    different ways.
We can serve each other well, despite our busy days.
Be patient. You are growing. Your world is growing,
    too.
Your questions will be answered when the time is
    right for you.

Scripture

Faith
Fits This is what the Gospel of Luke says about Jesus' growing
up in Nazareth:

> The child grew in size and strength. He was filled
> with wisdom, and the grace of God was with him.
> (2:40, INT)

Reflections

How are you different now from who you were two years
ago? How are you the same? How do you think you will
be two years from now?

What is one important lesson about life that you've
learned in the past two years?

What is one important lesson that you have learned
while reading this book?

Acknowledgments *(continued)*

The scriptural quotations marked NRSV are from the New Revised Standard Version of the Bible. Copyright © 1989 by the Division of Christian Education of the National Council of the Churches of Christ in the United States of America. All rights reserved.

The scriptural quotations marked NAB are from the New American Bible with revised Psalms and revised New Testament. Copyright © 1991, 1986, and 1970 by the Confraternity of Christian Doctrine, 3211 Fourth Street NE, Washington, DC 20017. All rights reserved.

The scriptural quotations marked INT are from The Inclusive New Testament: Co-sponsor's Edition (Brentwood, MD: Priests for Equality, 1994). Copyright © 1994 by Priests for Equality. All rights reserved.

The scriptural quotations marked GNB are from the Good News Bible with Deuterocanonicals/Apocrypha: The Bible in Today's English Version (New York: American Bible Society, 1978). Old Testament copyright © 1976, Deuterocanonicals/Aprocrypha copyright © 1979, New Testament copyright © 1966, 1971, 1976, by the American Bible Society.

The excerpts on pages 63, 76, and 82 are from *Scripture Readings: Advent to Pentecost* (Indianapolis: Carmelite Monastery, 1989), pages 349, 124, and 53, respectively. Copyright © 1989 by the Carmelites of Indianapolis.

The motto of the Christopher Society on page 68 is from *Familiar Quotations,* fourteenth edition, by John Bartlett, edited by Emily Morison Beck (Boston: Little, Brown and Company, 1968), page 981. Copyright © 1968 by Little, Brown and Company.

The excerpt on page 85 is from *The People's Catechism: Catholic Faith for Adults,* by William J. O'Malley, SJ; Mitch and Kathy Finley; Kathleen Hughes, RSCJ; Barbara Quinn, RSCJ; and Timothy E. O'Connell; edited by Raymond A. Lucker, Patrick J. Brennan, and Michael Leach (New York: Crossroad Publishing, 1995), page 26. Copyright © 1995 by The Crossroad Publishing Company.